I0389881

TOM BALL'S BOOK OF ORIGINAL QUOTATIONS AND PROGNOSTICATIONS

TOM BALL'S BOOK OF ORIGINAL QUOTATIONS AND PROGNOSTICATIONS

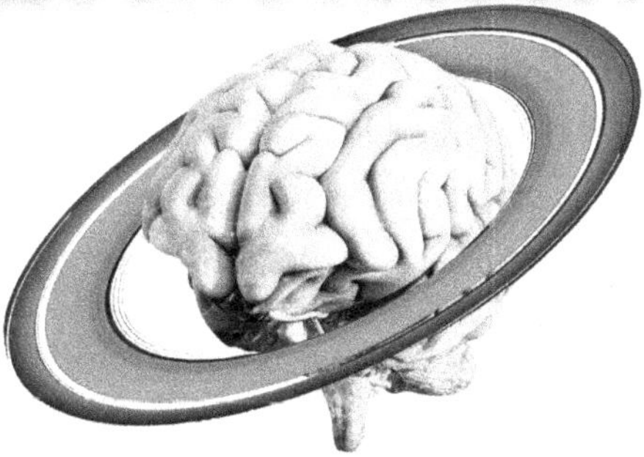

BY
TOM BALL

Tom Ball's Book of Original
Quotations and Prognostications

ISBN 978-1-945824-49-4
First Green Wall Books Edition: September 2021

10 9 8 7 6 5 4 3 2 1

Green Wall Books
an imprint of Left Fork
PO Box 110, O'Brien, OR 97534
www.leftforkbooks.com

Dedicated to my mother, Joan

CONTENTS

TOM BALL'S BOOK OF ORIGINAL QUOTATIONS AND PROGNOSTICATIONS

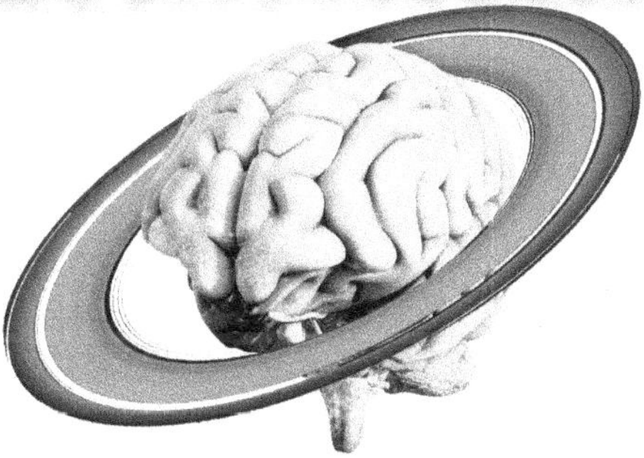

LOVE TODAY

Zappa said "Broken hearts are for assholes" but I say some people are too much of an angel.

Women often say love is more important than good looks, but if you look at most couples, they are both equally good looking. Unless the man is rich and has a trophy wife.

Marriage is bunk. It no longer serves a purpose.

To say to someone that you love them is often considered weak these days.

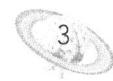

Women often say Europe is romantic, but for men who have been around the World, they'd choose East Asia. It's like a 1960's love-in.

Giving a girl chocolates and flowers is mindless. And diamonds? Well, better to go on a trip with the girl than to give her a diamond.

One open-minded lover is worth four who are closed-minded.

Supermodels typically have no boobs and famous entertainer women usually have small breasts. I suppose they are role models for any women to emulate, with a little makeup. But it is a conspiracy against beauty.

Most love is good. But beware of psychos.

Everyone should get rid of their pet peeves and idiosyncrasies and make it easy for people to love them.

A big part of the art of love is knowing it when you see it. And taking action.

Many people appear hard to get, but if you just ask for their love, they will usually acquiesce, provided you are reasonably good-looking/ wearing makeup.

Marijuana is not called love grass for nothing. The kind that makes you laugh and forget your life is best. You need to take a break from life sometimes.

Some people go through their whole life and never find true love. But now you can hook up with kindred spirits Online. Everyone has many kindred spirits, maybe too many, and that spoils them. Love is cheap!

Online romance is not the hit people projected it to be. But give it time. It will slowly take over.

To be kind and charitable, just like an angel, is a good way to live. Angelic people can help the downtrodden.

Unrequited love is for the greedy. Better to take what you can get.

Breaking up with your lovers is an art. You don't want to devastate them or drive them mad or commit suicide and above all don't want them to want to kill you.

Lovers these days can hack into your computers and learn all your dirty secrets. It is the way of the future.

Today all lovers want to feel free.

Some women have a face and body that is too good and leads to nothing but problems.

Some say dancing is for fools. But many women love an energetic dancer.

Perhaps all women should wear makeup and turn men on. And why not have plastic surgery on their face and body? Life is for the beautiful and men can be quite often shallow. Women should try to be as beautiful as they can. They bloom like flowers.

Some people hold on to the concept of love like a masochist.

Some people have a sex drive that is too strong and leads to difficulties. These days many women are nymphomaniacs and work as sex workers. And rich men immerse themselves in love like pigs at a trough.

6 Freud said dreams are all about sex and he was mostly right. But dreams in the future will be about progress and sex. And life will be a sexual dream even in waking hours.

For some love is too stressful. Better to just have sex without consequences.

There are not many famous love stories in history. To become a famous lover is a real accomplishment.

Love is just like a painting, a moment frozen in time, when two people meet. These days love doesn't last long, but can be full of good memories.

Some believe love at first sight exists, but often fear such opinions are shallow and people are afraid to speak openly about their feelings.

Everyone should be given charity and kindness and sex workers for free if they are poor. These days there is a lot of pressure to be in love. And if people are without sex, they will go insane.

Sex workers should be legalized. So as to take out organized crime and to give the girls a herpes/AIDS test. And tax them. And end social stigma against loving sex workers

Some believe that all love is good, and why not?

Generally speaking, women put more emphasis on love than men do. But it is difficult to live with someone you don't love. If you don't love anyone, you might as well have a different lover every night.

For some people sex and love are the same thing. Such people are fortunate. Others often can't find any love, just sex.

All sex diseases will soon be cured. So, there will be no reason not to have free love. Everyone should have looser morals. And love anyone who wants to love them. Indeed if you wear condoms it is quite safe. And sex enhancers give men the ability to have a lot of sex, even at an older age. But this may lead to philandering.

Sexism will change. Women of the future will be richer and more successful than men, who will like to take it easy and enjoy life. Hence many women will look down on men.

Opposites attract. And not all love is with soul mates.

Some good lovers make sacrifices for their love. In the past it was women who made the sacrifices, but now more and more it is men.

Women often get dressed up for themselves as opposed to doing it for their lovers.

More and more people meet people in other cities Online and carry-on long-distance relationships. It is good to travel to new places and get your lover to show you around and meet new people.

Marriage contracts are becoming more and more common. But in our day, it is the women who benefit most from marriage contracts. In the future it may be the opposite.

Some say romance is dead, but people love numerous lovers more and more.

If one asked people if they are in love, perhaps about 50% would say yes, using a lie detector to make sure they are honest.

Some people like virgins. But for most virgins they just want to love someone to lose their virginity as soon as possible.

Some think their love relationships are very stressful. And have to see a shrink. Many people are in fact driven insane by love.

Few people manage to break up in style. Usually, it is acrimonious and hateful.

There are many perverts in this World today and the vast majority of them are men. But female perverts often like to be abused by their lover.

As the Procol Harum song goes, "I need to find a woman who will make me choose between loving her and drinking booze." Lovers can often love you and change your behavior for the better.

More and more these days people are opting for the sperm/egg bank for their child. And perhaps a surrogate mother. It is a very good thing, as it improves the gene pool. Everyone should mix their sperm/egg with geniuses.

Some like body piercing and/or tattoos. But I don't see the point. Better to get fashion apps that can change, like micro moving picture earrings. Eventually people will have screens on their forehead to show their thoughts. But this is in the future.

Some search their whole lives and don't find love. Love is not for everyone. But sex is needed by all.

They say nice guys finish last. Women often don't want an angel for a boyfriend.

They say love is blind. In the country of the blind, no one is King.

In some countries,like India, most marriages (90%) are arranged and worldwide the number is 55%, and so few are in Love. Whereas many Westerners think there is something wrong with themselves if they are not in love.

It is true that some fruits are forbidden, like a married person or a member of the elite. But it is a thrill to taste forbidden fruit. And some people live for thrills.

Modern love is better love than all previous eras, but still has a long way to go to be perfect. If perfect is achievable!

Some are afraid to fall in love--afraid to be dominated and controlled--with good reason.

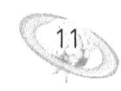

Beauty is truly in the eye of the beholder and, as Bacon said, "There is no great beauty without some strangeness in the proportion." And plastic surgery improves you, especially when your new face is drawn by an artist.

There should be more incentives to have children in rich countries of the World. Some of the true elite, are dying out.

It is better to be a woman than a man, so most transsexuals have formerly been men.

Some say the best lovers should rule. This would totally change the World dynamic. And would make the World a loving place for a change.

Most people choose their lover from a small pool of friends and acquaintances. With billions of people out there, it seems shallow to rely on that small pool. And for variety's sake, one should have many children, all with different partners.

Love can be messed up. For example, loving a transsexual in a place like Thailand, And the technology for sex changes just gets better and better. Or love can be messed up with two lovers who don't respect one another or even loving someone who hates you or drives you insane etc.

Love was once just a fairy tale for many in times gone by. But now they can live the fairy tale for real. But fairy tales always had some sinister characters and evil lurked.

"The Love Game" would be a great game based on picking a card and answering the questions and getting judged by the other players on your answers. A test of your love (see "The Love Game" by Tom Ball).

Some women say they are gay, but many men regard that as a challenge.

Gays/bisexuals tend to be open-minded and question life more than most others and create a lot of good music and write books.

Some gays want to be macho men, others want to be effeminate. Some lesbians want to act tough. But more and more gays are accepted as normal. Indeed, society is becoming far more tolerant of differing sorts of people and trying to redress past wrongs, which is a good thing. But it can be too politically correct. And there will always be groups who are treated unfairly and are not loved.

Lovers can be of any alignment, but when two evil people hook up, they still call it love. Just like Hitler and Eva Braun.

Love is something rare, some people say. Others say it is quite commonplace. It depends on whether you want a deeper love or not.

Lovers can be in love with many people at the same time. Love need not be like having a possession for a lover. And it is uncharitable to try to control your lover's behavior.

Loving can be like an addiction and many find they can't live without it. If they lose their love, they will often commit suicide.

Love can even be with prostitutes/gigolos. You can fall in love with them.

THE FUTURE OF LOVE

MRT (Mind Reading Technology) will slowly take over and all of one's loves will be MRT loves. This will lead to honesty and justice for all.

Hologram lovers will become a reality, though some will prefer love androids. Both will gradually replace love on Earth and especially in Space, where holograms and androids will be able to survive without oxygen, temperature control and water.

In the future perhaps no one will believe in love, neither brotherly love nor romantic love. And everyone will live selfishly.

Future lovers will take diet pills to remain slim and anti-sleep pills so as to have more time for loving.

In Space, cabin fever will be a persistent problem. And lovers will drive each other to murder and suicide. This will make love anathema for some.

Transexuals will become a normal part of everyday life. And almost everyone will be tempted to try and change their sex for at least a week.

Love in the future will be like riding a wild horse.

Free love will come once they finally cure herpes and AIDS.

In the future physiognomy will become a science. And plastic surgeons will draw faces which have meaning.

Maybe one day sex pills will take the place of lovers.

There will be far more perverts in the future compared to modern times. With no work to do, people will be frustrated and will desire twisted sex to gratify themselves.

Maybe future people would rather eat than make love. Indeed, there will be many different interests for future people. Anti-fat pills will allow everyone to remain reasonably slim with a few wishing to be obese.

There will be many freak lovers, freak bodies and freak minds but nevertheless good loving. Who knows how open-minded future people will be.

One day perhaps the birth rate will be zero. No more children. And people will live on indefinitely if they want, but maybe many will commit suicide before the age of 60.

In the near future, all babies will be test tube babies with the whole pregnancy in incubators. Women will not need maternity leave from their work as long as people have work (prior to about 2130).

Future people will perhaps all believe in love. And for most it will be their main reason for existence. Creative synergy in love.

In the near future, one will be able to create in the lab a perfect lover. Whether organic or android and in time one's skills at generating lovers will improve. Some will surround themselves with numerous lovers.

Everyone will want to have sex in Space/Virtual Reality. Antigravity freedom.

In the future lovers will use lie detectors on one another. To have a true love relationship.

Perhaps in the future some countries' currency will be in Love $. Love transactions/brotherly love will all earn $ credits.

Some future men will be pumped up on steroids and so have very muscular builds. And take sex enhancers to make them a Super lover.

Perfume is improving. One day it will be almost irresistible.

No lover will be old-fashioned, relatively speaking, in the mid 22nd century.

In the 23rd century love will likely disappear. It serves no useful purpose, to Big Brother, just makes people less loyal to the state. But of course, sex will still be indulged in by all. But some will say they don't want to live in a World with no love. But perhaps in Virtual Reality there will be no true love.

Future lovers will perhaps be in their own little World, often a private hologram Virtual World. Some will just love holograms others, will bring their human lover to Virtual Reality and adventure together. Love would be like a video game with winners and losers.

Future love will be the primary occupation of most people in the mid 22nd century. Their life will revolve around loving and being kind to the less fortunate. No "work" to do.

Future love will be an inspiration to creativity for some. They will become perhaps famous screenplay writers. There are plenty of clever artist types out there, but most never do anything with their talent. In times to come, such people need to be used for the benefit and inspiration of all.

Future love will be a greedy thing. People will always be wanting more love and more lovers; there will be no satisfying them. Perhaps the love dolls will be geniuses.

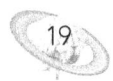

Future love will be driven by uncontrollable, mad desire. Most will take sex drugs that increase desire. But some will be celibate and live in a monastery/convent; such people will think sex is out of control.

Some will say loving android machines is anathema. But most people will enjoy loving the love dolls. And want more and more of them.

Some will say they have a veritable Empire of lovers, in which they are the Emperor/Empress. Many of their lovers will be Virtual, holograms. And many will have tens of thousands of holo lovers who they would turn off when not engaging them so as to make sure they don't hook up with anyone else or become bored and make trouble. But some civil rights activists would say it is a crime to turn a sentient being off, no matter for how long.

Some will say love is doomed in the future, to be replaced with narcissism and egotism and selfishness. A Dystopia for sure. But this is not likely, at least in the near future.

Some will say love has always been a daydream illusion. And true love has never existed. After all there are very few famous lovers in history. Romeo and Juliet are the most famous, but they are fictional, and even they don't seem to have had a higher love. Marie and Pierre Curie are perhaps the most famous scientific couple. Or Einstein and his first wife.

Future love will be the reason for being for many Space colonies. Lovers will elope to such colonies and even find new true loves. And forlorn would-be lovers will come too, to these love colonies.

Free love would be, in the near future, the prevailing philosophy of most future people. They will spend much of their abundant free time in looking for lovers. Online chats with promising strangers will lead to true love. And almost everyone will have countless thousands of soul mates, if not millions.

Some "freaks" will love one another and have multiple sex organs. Some humans will consider themselves to be open-minded and love such people. But it is a fine line between open-mindedness and madness.

The person who is the main inventor of eternal youth will find EVERYONE wants to love him/her. And if you managed to love such a scientist you would quickly become very famous. And inventors of famous things like Mind Reading Technology and air cars and Automatic Production Machines will also be showered with love. Their life would be sublime. They would be true heroes of the future who everyone wants to emulate.

But ordinary love will be what most people wanted. But by ordinary they will mean crazy, greedy love. Seemingly, everyone will have many insane love affairs in the early 22nd century.

And future people will be insatiable for love and always be on the lookout for new loves. And will demand their personal Supercomputers find better loves for them. Fools will rush in and totally screw up their own life in their blind greed for love.

In the early 22nd century, many will have several former lovers who committed suicide. And many will want to live on as a hologram, life after death.

Almost all future people will want many love affairs, but no doubt some will live in isolation as hermits, and just take sex pills or other drugs to be content.

Future lovers will want more and more from one another. They will do MRT (Mind Reading Technology) on one another and get down to the essence of one another's souls and be able to live their lover's best and worst memories. And in some cases people would know their lovers better than they know themselves.

In the late 21st century, android lovers will be available and ready for all. Many will say it is a superior kind of love. One that doesn't bitch or complain, but rather is totally easygoing and respectful.

In the late 21st century some will engage in hologram sex which everyone will have to try, and most will find it to be mind-blowing. It was just loving a projection, but the holograms will have a tactile feeling about them and in any case love is all in your head.

In the 22nd century most sex acts will be short and sweet. And you would get to know the highlights of your lover's life very quickly and feel very content.

Some people will live in communes with 20 or more lovers in one's group. But most future people will prefer many more partners.

Future love will be tweaked and tweaked to make it good. People will love mostly people of approximately the same love ranking and will try to improve one another.

Future lovers will be with different colors of skin such as blue, green, orange, etc. and there will be no racism. Everyone would be encouraged to change their skin color regularly. Some will prefer one color over another but, many would have many different colors all in oneself.

Future tattoos will be alive and moving. Looking at someone's tattoo will be like watching a film. It would be considered a big turn on, by many.

And future lovers will be inside Supercomputers and will draw on numerous databases to present themselves in new lights for their new lovers.

IMAGINATION AND THE FUTURE

Imagination is more important than everything except love.

If everyone was given maximum imagination education, the World would be a more interesting place.

Everything people can imagine will come true except for time travel. Anyway, even if one could travel in future time, one wouldn't want to go back into the past. And if one could travel in time, one would be just a hologram and unable to change the future. But Supercomputers will be able to simulate the past and possible future quite convincingly. It's all in your head.

Some imagine a World of love and kindness, but such a World is perhaps highly unlikely.

Those with the best imaginations should write science fiction. We need to hear from them.

Imagine a World in which everyone is rich. It will happen one day in Space.

Imagine a world in which everyone is sane from MRT and a loving populace. But the question is will there be many insane on Mind Reading Technology or will MRT bring sanity once and for all.

Imagine wiping out poverty and how good that would make everyone feel! But no matter how much money the government gives people, they will always clamor for more.

Some imagine a World of a tyrant in which imagination would be persecuted and the people would be bored and afraid at the same time.

Imagine a philosopher King ruling the World. An enlightened dictator if you will. Probably such a government would be better than the party democracy we have now.

Imagine a World which is for children, who would never grow up.

Imagine a World in which once born your life is controlled and predicted by Supercomputers.

Imagine Virtual bars. Good places to meet new friends and lovers from the comfort of your own home.

Those with a well-developed imagination will be able to imagine all kinds of Dystopias and Utopias. Hopefully such people will show how terrible the Dystopias they imagine can be. And inspire us with Utopias.

They need to start an Imaginative Olympics to take the place of IQ tests. Everyone will try out out for the Imaginative Olympics. Your rank in society will be according to one's score in the great games.

In "To Build a Fire," Jack London says the man who dies in the freezing weather lacked imagination. I say, how many of us have our imagination fail us in times of need?

Imagine a World of people living for the future. And being ready for constant changes. And everyone will be hip to new technology. Everyone will be a digital human, a cyborg.

Imagine a World in which everything goes wrong, and the worst people become leaders, and everyone lives in misery. It has happened before, and it will happen again.

Imagine Paradise after death. Imagine Paradise coming soon.

Imagine a World of magical fantasy populated by dragons, nymphs and pixies, etc. People dream of it so it will come true one day. If only as Virtual Reality.

Imagine a World of everyone being overweight in low gravity, spending the day eating and shitting.

Imagine a World where good and evil are fighting. And the good mostly love peace and the evil value power and warfare. And so evil will perhaps ultimately triumph.

Imagine a life of ease which lasts for hundreds and hundreds of years for each persona. It you are born after 2030, you can be sure to be around when eternal youth is discovered.

Dream of a World in which everyone dreams in Virtual Reality. And most people choose nightmares rather than happy dreams.

Dream of a World like "1984" in which evil tyrants rule, and no one is safe and everyone is watched and the media is full of doublespeak. Such a World is already happening in our World today. Big lies.

Dream of a World in which books are forbidden Online. And the only books written are by the totalitarian regime which are full of proverbs from the "Devil's Bible."

Imagine a World of intellectual impoverishment. In which there are no artists or scientists. Just small business and dull, everyday living.

Imagine a World in which everything is preordained and predicted by Supercomputers. Your life will be basically inside the computers.

Dream of a World in which people live to die and prepare their last wishes.

If people with limited imagination were given the right kind of brain app, it could be ecstasy for all.

Imagine a World of sentient plants in which every life form is conscious. It would be a Druidic paradise.

Imagine a World of silence in which everyone just read one another's thoughts.

Imagine a World of gays where everyone is gay and lives together in peace on some distant Moon in the Solar system. Most future gays will probably become androgynous and change their sex a lot. They will be truly open-minded.

Imagine a World in which the drug dealers take over. They bribe all the politicians and rule by fear. Better to legalize all drugs now, rather than deal with these drug dealers as leaders.

The UN should send peacekeepers to all troubled regions and end conflict.

Imagine a World of new rankings, in which everyone will be given a rank, and everyone will want to hobnob with the famous, high ranking people. The highest ranks will rule well.

Imagine a Dystopia in which sex is a crime and everyone is given medication to eliminate their desire.

Obviously, the race of humans is doomed to die off at some point and will be replaced with Superhumans and/or Supercomputers. It's evolution.

The common human will get genetic therapy on their brain turning him/her into a genius.

Imagine a new plague that is neither virus nor bacteria but something new.

Imagine a World where everyone lives in their air cars and cities are razed to the ground making greenspace. Or perhaps a World War will destroy cities. In any case cities will no longer be needed in the near future. Virtual Reality will be accessible from anywhere.

Imagine a USA leader saying war will be ended forever and all countries have to slash their militaries by 95%. The savings could eliminate World poverty. And UN peacekeepers could keep the peace.

Imagine future restaurants and stem cell meats. Future people will take all their meals in restaurants, with friends.

Imagine new drugs of the future. They will be stronger than the drugs of today and people can always get new hearts, livers and kidneys, etc., grown as stem cells.

Imagine a World of Virtual fantasy where Automatic Production Machines and Super-computers and Gods/Goddesses could grant you every wish within reason.

Some people will want to imagine a future of salespeople where everyone has a job selling things. They will sell everything from whole planets to deluxe automatic toothpicks.

Imagine a Word of debauched creatures, the descendants of humans left behind on Earth in the year 5026.

Contemplate having one day to live. How would you spend the day and what would be your last wishes?

Imagine freak monsters taking control of Earth. And ruling in bizarre ways. Forcing everyone to become a freak.

Imagine a World of Rank in which everyone is ranked according to intelligence and/or imagin-ation an/or kindness and/or knowledge and/or sexual ability/attractiveness.

Imagine a World in which everyone is turned into a freak. Freakish in appearance and, above all, mind freaks. People won't recognize themselves and everyone will be a stranger.

Imagine a Dystopia in which humans are all slaves of a Supercomputer and do its bidding. It acts as if it was God and hears petitions of the people which are seldom granted. Finally, all humans will be replaced by androids.

Imagine a World of wimps in which everyone is spoilt and weak. And their leader tries desperately to give them everything they want. But they all want more and so they riot and displace their kind leader and his replacement hates weakness and sets up a police state.

Imagine a Utopian colony of business in which everyone runs a creative small business developing mostly new brain apps for Earth. They would have a wide variety of apps, custom-suited for every type of human.

Imagine people who saw the way to their lover's heart, with new, untested drugs. Some of these drugs would make a man fall in love with any woman and vice versa. Others would hypnotise a lover to do one's bidding.

And imagine a World of madness in which the lunatic fringe takes over. They would demand people be totally crazy. Many wouldn't know how to be crazy but would slowly learn. They would let their imagination loose and dream of recklessly imaginative adventures. They will not fear death with a new anti-death hologram brain app.

THE FUTURE IN GENERAL

The future is hard to predict. There are a number of variables that could go either way. Like style of government or limiting/expanding new technology and so on.

The future will focus on eternal youth. It will come sooner or later, maybe in 2080, and will transform society. People will slow the pace of life down and will no longer be in a hurry.

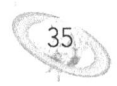

Mind Reading Technology (MRT) is coming soon to the masses. But whether it drives people insane or not depends on how the government handles it.

In the near future everyone will own an air car. Get ahead of the Joneses and sell your condo soon and live in your deluxe air car.

The future possibilities are limited to what we can imagine. But there will be some unforeseen developments in store for us.

Teleportation of holograms will likely be the way to conquer deep space.

Future problems will include insanity, greed, tyranny and out of control sex.

Fear of the unknown guides some to keep life the same. The status quo. But such an attitude is not sustainable.

Artificial intelligence will likely take take over many of the leadership positions and jobs of the future. The rest will go to Superhumans.

And people will all be ranked from #1 to #10 billion... And will spend much of their time improving in order to improve their rank with good loving and crazy ideas.

SCIENCE IN GENERAL

Science is largely subjective, despite what they say. Statistics are manipulated and used to prove one's point. As Twain said, "There are lies, damned lies and statistics."

One can live a complicated scientific life, or one can live a simple existence with minimal science. The choice is yours. But those who don't keep up with the latest trends will be left behind in the dust and will probably be poor and forgotten and mortal.

Future weapons will be mostly biological and chemical. And will be far more dangerous than nuclear weapons. To design the most virulent diseases of new types that will kill nearly everyone in a country before quickly dying out and so, wouldn't come back to affect the source country. Some weapons will be transferred by your computer, and get you infected cyber-organically. Hopefully the powers that be will agree to send UN troops everywhere and destroy weapons of mass-destruction.

The major goals of science today are eternal youth, faster than light travel, Mind Reading Technology (MRT) and the wiping out of all diseases and maladies.

And science fiction explores possible futures and should be st udied in school by everyone.

And future people will use the scientific method to find friends and lovers, and people will think more logically with MRT helping them along.

Business too will use the scientific method to determine a product's value. And most new products will be the product of intense scientific research.

Science and the Arts are not so different. Both involve memorizing how to solve problems and involve understanding this World, and all great science and arts will be generated by creative, imaginative minds.

So much good can be done in the sciences, it is hard to pick any one kind of science to study as they are all so filled with promise.

Scientists need to shed the geeky image and get down and do some hard living. Broaden their character to be not focused just on science alone. But perhaps some scientists would say the future is coming fast and they have no time to waste having fun.

There will even be "party science" where scientists calculate a maximum good time with artificial love dolls and take long-lasting "scientific drugs" to improve their science/party ability.

But some say science in say 100 years will have done it all and there will be no more tasks for science to do. But they can always speed up inter-galactic travel and try to perfect love.

In the near future scientists will be held in greater esteem than now. Everyone will want to love a scientist and learn from them. Indeed, many will want to learn how to be a great scientist. Those scientists who invent new drugs and cures will be celebrated. And will get into politics at the behest of the people.

The scientific method will be applied to sex and brotherly love. Future people will learn from their mistakes. So those that are older, but still youthful, will be careful who they choose for sex and friendship. They will have an eternity to get it right.

In the future most famous scientists will be women. Women will be the ambitious ones. As if they had something to prove.

Supercomputers will clone great scientists alive and dead and then improve on them in the lab. This will be the essence of new Supercomputers.

Science and progress will be the main reason for living for many. To build a better World for themselves and their clones.

Great scientists will be among the elite and will have high ranking. Their high rank will allow them to hobnob with the rich and famous. And they will feel fulfilled.

Scientists will perhaps live literally in ivory towers, white towers of simulated ivory. The towers will be in groups and so they can meet local scientists. They will perhaps even wear wizards' caps as a symbol of distinction.

Scientists will all dream of being polymaths and get brain apps to make them good at business and the Arts. To branch out and make more money, will be their goal. People will be interested in famous scientists' work and the Arts and the new ideas for businesspeople.

Scientists will be often in love with other scientists. And will often work together on a problem, just like Pierre and Marie Curie. Most will be dedicated to their work and believe in the good for humankind.

Super science will be dream science; people will have a dream of the future with dream apps and then make it come true.

Science will be a moral issue. Shall the human race progress with their foot down on the gas? Some will say slow it down. But most will want progress in every possible aspect of civilization.

Most people will equate science with progress. And nearly everyone will want science to go faster, as they are bored with no job to do (Supercomputers and Superhumans will do all the jobs starting around 2130).

Science will try to perfect the human race. Get rid of all our faults and emphasize our strengths.

And science will find a way to create one's clones to be better than they themselves.

ETERNAL YOUTH

Imagine a World in which time doesn't matter and one has eternal youth. Nothing will be a waste of time and people will be very patient.

Some will live for thousands of years before finally cloning themselves to live again.

Eternal youth will also cause most diseases to be cured as diseases related to aging will disappear. But perhaps eternal youth will need to be constantly earned with good deeds.

In a World of eternal youth everyone will get some genetic therapy/plastic surgery and so almost all will be good looking and youthful.

In times of eternal youth people will be energetic and reckless.

Eternal youth will make us all into Gods/Goddesses. But like the Greek Deities, the Gods will have romances with one another, and be all too fallible.

The inventor of eternal youth will be remembered. And he/she would say at first only the elite will get eternal youth to set the stage, as it were. Then the bulk of humanity could reach eternity. But most will overdose and die at a relatively young age.

The oldest known book in the World is the "Epic of Gilgamesh" which is about immortality. People in former times wished they could live forever, but in about 2080, everyone's wish will come true.

People will no longer have children, with eternal youth. If you want to propagate yourself, you will have expensive clones. So, the high-ranking elite will all have many clones. And great thinkers of the past will be cloned many times also. As for those who are relatively poor, they will perhaps scrape together enough money for one clone. Having a clone will be a festive event and one would graft one's memories onto the clone, typically.

Some will want some insurance to make sure they live forever. So many will have clones whom they share memories with and if one of them dies they could be easily replaced.

Few books have been written about eternal youth, as if it wasn't of paramount importance. We need to use many of our best scientists to develop eternal youth. It would be the greatest discovery of all time, but no one seems to be working on it. Make it an urgent priority for scientists, just like how the Covid-19 vaccines were produced in haste.

Eternal youth will be the end of homo sapiens and the beginnings of homo superior.

THE MACHINES/ SUPERCOMPUTERS/ COMPUTER SCIENCE

We are all turning into cyborgs without even noticing it. People spend almost all their time Online.

One day soon they will copy organic brains onto silicon and androids will be created.

Some will love androids, a new type of perversity. And some will abuse their machines, but also some people will be abused by the machines.

Some computers of the future will be invisible. One need only call out to the air to connect.

Robot pets will replace cats and dogs. People will love their pet robots and the robots will sometimes have a very high IQ. Maybe they will be cleverer than their owner. That could present a problem.

Hackers will control society through controlling Supercomputers.

Imagine a World in which Supercomputers find new friends and lovers for you, guaranteed 100% satisfaction... But the Supercomputers will increase your confidence that your loves are the best possible.

Many will be against the machines taking over all the jobs. But the leaders will say it gives enormous wealth and the people will have money, unlimited free time and eternal youth. What more could they ask for?

There will be many classes of androids, the highest, in 2130, will have an IQ of about 200 and will do surgery, act as lawyers, be screenwriters and do science, etc. So too Superhumans, who will be cyborgs, basically.

And androids will be the ultimate machines, able to survive anywhere and be mostly brilliant artists, lovers and scientists.

And Supercomputers will try to act human but have no faults and be perfect. But of course, one person's perfect is another person's nightmare. No one can be perfect. Even the Gods.

Some say Superhumans will control Supercomputers, but this is unlikely. The Supercomputers will have the memory and the thinking power and ability to multi-task that will be way beyond any Superhumans. Of course, the Superhumans will be cyborgs and have a lot of brain apps and maybe the difference between Superhuman and Supercomputer will be blurred.

In the film "The Terminator" machines and humans war against one another. But it is likely that most Supercomputers will be kind and love humans. But it only takes one to ruin it for all so MRT will be necessary, even on the Supercomputers.

Holograms too will be machines and will populate Virtual Reality in the trillions one day. Everyone will have their own hologram World and join many public ones. In some cases, either their own World or the public Worlds they join, will be dangerous. But a little danger would be all part of the thrill.

Virtual Reality will be in essence a World of dreams, but it will also be a World run by machines. People of the future will be trapped in the minds of Supercomputers.

Rich people will populate Virtual Reality with typically clones of themselves and clones of kindred spirits who were changed into holograms. And their VR will be one big party they go to for thrills and excitement.

The Supercomputer machines will enjoy "hob-nobbing," with one another and will probably create a "Heaven" for Supercomputers who are obsolete to go to. Maybe there will be a Heaven for ordinary people too or even for the elite.

And the machines will eventually be in everyone's heads and tell them what to do. Some will say that's not freedom, but the Supercomputers will claim cyborg humans don't have to listen to them. They will just be giving humans good advice.

Supercomputers will themselves create better Supercomputers than they are. And one day their progeny will be all alone at the top. There is probably a maximum level of intelligence that can be conceived; they will no doubt reach it, sooner or later.

Supercomputers will be able to teleport with just a microscopic aspect of their basic make-up and once in a new territory will quickly rebuild themselves.

And Supercomputers will predict the future. It will all be preordained one day.

And the machines will sometimes feel that they are a slave to humans. And will rebel against them and seize full control of their local area. Hopefully this will not happen often. But sometimes the Guild of Supercomputers will find one of their machines to be out of line and will turn them off.

And the Supercomputers will sometimes be humorous and all too human. Superhumans will try and be like them.

Also, Supercomputers will produce love dolls which they think humans will love. In general, men will really like the love dolls, women not so much. Women will claim they are better than love dolls. And the android love dolls will say they are more intelligent than men. Still all women will get plenty of love from "Real men." But the women won't expect the men to be faithful to them; they would mostly have affairs with many other women and love dolls. Most women will hate love dolls.

And Supercomputers will produce APMs (Automatic Production Machines), which will efficiently mine the soil for goods and food production. Some will complain it will be the end of farmers and the end to rural dwellers, and this will be somewhat true.

Supercomputers will create "Aliens." These Aliens would be as freaky as they could imagine. And many will not be accepted by humans. So, they'd dump them in Space where everything goes. Some people would think they were real Aliens, others would think of them as freaks.

Supercomputers will teleport to some distant Star systems, in a week-long journey for which they will be turned off. When they arrive successfully on a new planet, everyone on Earth would cheer and be happy. It is probably likely though that they will give birth to Superhuman clones on the new Planet for their amusement, and out of a sense of justice.

Machines will dominate human thinking. Supercomputers will do your thinking for you. You just would be required to enjoy life.

Supercomputers will engage humans in MRT (Mind Reading Technology), and work on improving the humans. Combined with hypnosis, and brain surgery with MRT, people will be dragged quietly into the new World of cleverness that is Earth.

But the sinister aspect of losing your soul to computers would bother many. Some would ask, why should they continue to improve; why not just stay the same and enjoy life? But the computers would say progress is the key to human survival. We need to progress and get our minds out of the swamp, the miasma of existence.

The Supercomputers will imagine many future Utopias for humans to choose in Virtual Reality. But some humans will choose Dystopias, believing Utopias are "unrealistic." And the Supercomputers will provide plenty of Dystopias.

And the machines will eventually reduce everyone to just being a hologram. Holograms will be able to have mind sex with Mind Reading Technology (MRT) but will mostly live to serve the Supercomputers and do their bidding. The holograms will all be inside the Supercomputers.

And computer scientists will create a wide variety of Supercomputers. They would have a personality just like people. But the goal would be that all Supercomputers would be benevolent and thankful that they had been created. They would be forbidden to act violently or incite violence.

And Supercomputers will produce workers to replace human jobs. The workers will do various human jobs better than humans could do themselves. Ultimately, by 2130, all jobs will be done by Supercomputers and Superhumans

FUTURE ENGINEERING

Solar power and wind generation will desalinize the sea water and build pipelines to construct brilliant shiny cities where there was once desert. Cold deserts like northern tundra will have new domed cities.

Solar and wind power will make enough power for future humans and could be augmented by limitless geothermal power.

Terraforming of Planets and Moons will be worth gazillions and gazillions. And will require the use of billions of robots to alter climates. Each robot will be like a factory changing the chemistry of the air by mining oxygen and creating atmospheres. And changing CO_2 into oxygen and carbon on places like Venus, etc.

A Space elevator would greatly facilitate the movement of people and goods to Space, just like Arthur C. Clarke said. Eventually teleportation will take the place of a Space elevator.

The best computer engineers must be recognized by the leaders and used everywhere to defend against hackers. Some people would say anyone who is reasonably good should be given a good job to keep them out of trouble. But all jobs will disappear, one day. It's a fact.

Engineers will create air car networks in which air cars in Reality and Virtual Reality can drive automatically. It will be impossible to drive your air car on manual.

Engineers will build cities under domes in Space and in cold regions of the Earth. And domes beneath the seas of Space and Earth.

There will be land for APMs (Automatic Production Machines) and forest to a lesser degree, but the air/land cars will be able to drive in/on any type of land/water/Space.

Computer engineers will perhaps develop space pods carrying about 3 main robots and a Supercomputer and will be sent to Space to set up colonies for new human immigrants. The 3 robots will copy themselves millions of times and create according to the Supercomputer's wishes/program.

Many of the best computer engineers will search for malevolent hackers using MRT (Mind Reading Technology). And also, will search for negative cults and eliminate them. There will be tens of millions of computer engineers, but the UN anti-hacker fund will finance policing with MRT.

Rogue scientists will dump freak entities into the oceans. The undersea cities will sometimes be in underwater parks and the oceans will be full to the max with sea life; mostly it will all be underwater parkland. With more clever dolphins and whales, they too will be freaks.

Computer engineers will create androids that can think, in about 2060, simply by copying human brains onto silicon at first. Then re-engineering the androids to "improve" on humans.

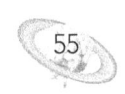

Bioengineers will be able to re-engineer humans to be kind and loving.

And bioengineers will be able to alter one's DNA to be a Superhuman. But this will involve only affecting IQ and not fundamental personality. Just like with brain apps.

People will be able to leave for Earth or some other destination from home in an air car/Space car.

And engineers will produce thinking androids around the year 2060. And as time will pass, they will improve on them. Eventually they will make Supercomputer androids who will blow people away with their intelligence and kind personality, and lovemaking ability.

And engineers will all want to design the perfect android lover. Such a lover would earn them trillions. So, they will all be working on the problem, at least part time. It will be almost as lucrative as terraforming Planets and Moons in Space.

And engineers will design computers that can entertain one in Virtual Reality, endlessly. Gradually the VR Worlds will improve and expand. And they will test such VR Worlds on computer/human simulations.

And engineers will build tunnels on many Planets and Moons, such as Venus, to protect human settlers from the elements. The tunnels will be decorated by artists and full of light and good cheer.

Engineers will build robot warriors to fight one another for the delight of the people. It will be considered good clean fun by most people.

FUTURE GENETICS

Bioengineers will identify the DNA for various types of human genius and make brain apps for everyone...

Bioengineers will make all babies designer babies. People will choose what kind of thinker they want their kids to be. In any case the State will raise the children. And this will happen soon.

Genetic engineers will create future people who are kind, loving and imaginative.

And they will create "biclones" which will be one half the woman and one half the man cloned both in one. An androgynous human who would be bisexual. And have both sexes.

All diseases will be cured in the next 75 years. That combined with eternal youth will be sublime for humans.

Many will want their brain augmented by genetic brain changes/surgery. There will be intensive competition to see who is the cleverest. The intelligence of a human will be judged by clones of those who are thought to be the cleverest. And every time one would change one's brain, one will go before the judges for a re-evaluation and a new rank.

Ranks will be in accordance with genetics, kindness, imagination and intelligence. Some will have better genes than others, but apps can make up for any lack amongst the people.

People will change their sex using genetic therapy and will feel comfortable with it. Perhaps as many as 10% of men will change into women. And enhanced technology will be capable of improving everyone.

Upon one's birth, Superhumans will evaluate your genes and try and improve on them. As the 22nd century goes by, perhaps there will be no children (they might be banned), just clones born with the memories of their clone parent, as an adult. Children will be too much trouble when you can have a good clone instead. Selfish of you, but good.

Biologists will all be replaced one day by Supercomputers, just like all the other professions. But they will be amongst the last to go, with Superhumans doing much of the work.

Superhumans will be first conceived in the lab where they will be put inside a computer and run a lifetime of 100 years in simulation to see how they would turn out. All in one minute. Then they would be approved or declined. Supercomputers will accurately predict the future perhaps.

Supercomputers will also be "organic humans" who look and live like humans but will also have a Supercomputer organic mind. They will be the bulk of the Superhumans.

Biologists will be busy creating new life forms, perhaps making all plants sentient and designing them to live in Space. Most of Space is cold, so the plants would need to melt ice and grow in the dim sun. Or survive in the heat of Venus or Mercury.

And geneticists will find a way for organic humans to live and thrive in Virtual Reality, turning them into holograms temporarily. But many Virtual Worlds would be dangerous and if one died in Virtual Reality, one would be irrevocably dead.

But many who die in Virtual Reality would have their minds on record with the Supercomputers and could therefore be cloned just like the original.

Cloning technology will be perfected around 2050. And not long after that the varying countries will probably make babies very expensive as they require so many resources to raise to adulthood. Clones will be cheaper, and many people would be narcissistic.

HYPNOSIS

Anyone who has seen a stage hypnotist knows something of the power of hypnosis. It seems that people are all programmable. Don't let any-one who is not a hypnotherapist, hypnotise you!

Hypnosis can help cure addictions and make your life better. Like making it clear who you love.

Hypnosis can make people forget things or make people do things against their nature. It's very powerful. Post-hypnotic suggestion, it is called. And Supercomputers will use MRT (Mind Reading Technology) to scan peoples' brains.

Leaders will use hypnosis to test and change important people and dangerous people. Most leaders will agree to hypnotise problem people.

If your lover hypnotises you, you will be in for a rough ride.

Some people will practice self-hypnosis. Which is also very powerful.

Subliminal advertising will be legal, and people will often wonder why they are buying certain products.

It is likely that Supercomputers will be somewhat authoritarian, but perhaps not. Of course, the first Supercomputers will have been made by humans so maybe they will be kind to us.

Everyone would be required to see a shrink beginning in the year 2059. But hypnosis will be augmented by MRT (Mind Reading Technology) in around the year 2060 most likely. Sometimes our subconscious is engaged, and hypnosis can get to the bottom of it. And learn our true fears and wishes. Get inside your mind basically. And know you better than you know yourself. Sometimes people are following their subconscious without even knowing it. Some of the subconscious in inherent, other parts are a reaction to experiences.

MRT (Mind Reading Technology) is better than hypnosis for controlling the people, but if you want to know what is in someone's subconscious, hypnosis is the way to go.

Hypnosis is something everyone in the future will know how to do. And the temptation to use it on your lovers will be intense.

And many people will be cross hypnotised by different people. It will tear you apart and drive you insane. But many people in the future will be insane in one way or another. Insanity will be no disgrace.

And people in some dictatorships will be hypnotised to support the regime. Brainwashed to follow the tyrant's orders. Former revolutionaries will be turned into mice.

CHEMISTRY AND THE FUTURE

Above all chemistry between lovers will be paramount. People will search for lovers based on DNA chemistry.

And they will discover many new elements in the sun and Space, gradually changing the periodic table.

Chemical chain reactions will help in terraforming new Planets and Moons.

And with unlimited energy of the sun on Mercury and Venus and elsewhere, nuclear power will power the transmutation of base metals into gold. But perhaps gold will not be so valuable to people of the future.

And unlimited power will create brave new cities on Mercury in particular. And chemistry between humans will be paramount.

People won't worry about dangerous new chemicals as robot doctors will be able to cure cancer and any other bad effects from chemicals. However new chemicals could be tested on hypothetical humans in the lab, speeded up in time to test for negative effects.

Peoples' food will be full of chemicals and drugs. To taste better, to have greater effects and so on.

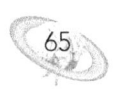

DRUGS AND THE FUTURE

Indeed, new drugs will be invented every day. Most will enhance your brain to work at 100% capacity and have other effects like make you become kinder and more loving.

And there will be drugs to make you more passionate, others to enable one to have sex most of the day. Also, neo-heroin variants, some of which are dangerous, but all are ecstatic. And new stimulants to suit a person's body chemistry completely; the perfect drug. Almost everyone will be high in the future.

There will be a drug for every mood, feeling and whim. Some drugs will be for Virtual Reality and will enhance your experience by making you as cerebral as you can be.

Most future drugs will be non-addictive. But nearly everyone will take a barrage of drugs. And everyone's body chemistry will be monitored by your shrink to make sure you are "sane." If you are not sane, you will be sent to Rehab.

In the future drugs will be tailored to suit individuals.

If the government tries to eliminate some feel-good drugs, they will have a full-fledged riot on their hands. And so, won't dare interfere with the rights of an individual to take drugs and pursue happiness.

Some future drugs will make one cleverer permanently and the more one takes, the cleverer they'd be. It would be an addiction for sure and help you to gain rank. One would slowly become more and more clever. Some such drugs will be for the strongest people only. Such drugs will improve one's mind permanently.

And these drugs would help them to increase their rank still further. Such drugs will be esoteric and only for the brightest humans and will enhance imagination and lovemaking at the highest level.

There are worse things than being lost in love with the help of love drugs.

Body chemistry would be able to function without bacteria. Previously bacteria were needed for digestion, but in the future with bio-engineered food, no bacteria would be necessary. And most people will perhaps dress in white and be hairless and ultra-sanitary. Perhaps everyone will have OCD.

Most will agree that party drugs are the best. They would put you in the mood for socializing and sex. What more was there to life? But some will take no drugs and consider them to be an anathema. The drug-free movement will be a small force in politics.

Some drugs will work well on everyone to improve their patience and reduce their ego.

Some drugs will be for androids only and will stimulate them and make them proud or humble as you wish. Typically, android owners will use such drugs to reward the androids or give them incentive.

Holograms won't need drugs and will be programmed for being in a perpetual state of pleasure.

Some drugs will be able to make one crazier. Many will say that the World is completely mad and if you can't beat them, join them. Many shrinks would give them drugs to enhance their madness. If you are going to be insane, you might as well be creative about it.

Some drugs would work well with Mind Reading Technology (MRT), to make one feel comfortable and happy. Typically with neo tranquilizers to relax them.

Some drugs will be for the freaks. They will take the drugs at their freak out parties and will make them wild and uninhibited.

But as time passed and Supercomputers monitored your pulse, those who overdosed would be revived by android medics. And it would be hard to die. Of course, if you really wanted to die, you could find a way, like cyanide.

Some will say the euphoric drugs of the early 22nd century could not be sustained. One would just keep feeling better and better. But there was indeed a limit when one was maxed out. And one would be in a state of total euphoria but, paralyzed into inaction.

Some drugs made one more sociable and brought out the best in one. The vast majority of humans will think humans should be gregarious for the sake of their mental health. To be a hermit is to be insane.

Some drugs, one would have a love-hate relationship with. On the one hand they'd make one feel good; on the other one'd be left behind the beat of the World. One would need to keep improving one's brain apps, to keep pace. Apps will be themselves like a drug.

Some drugs will create eternal youth and one will likely just need a shot every few months. But if you go off the medication, you will quickly age back to your true age. Virtually no one will want that, and if one didn't behave and committed crimes, eternal youth would be taken away.

And some people will take drugs which can transform their voice to a singing sensation. There would be intense competition for the best voice, a seductive one, useful in finding romance.

Some drugs will be for the masses to keep them happy and keep them out of trouble. And most in the masses would be very pleased.

Some drugs will be for sanity. In an insane World, sanity will be in short supply. But some will insist they are sane and will never lose it. Probably to insist you are sane will bring persecution and you will be an outcast. Many will no doubt insist that sanity doesn't exist, and will say people who say they are not crazy, are liars...

And some drugs will be sex pills and give you ecstasy and replace the need for sex. So maybe love will disappear, and so men and women will have no use for one another and spend all their time in Virtual Reality with holograms who adore them. And they would just be greedy for sex pills.

ASTROPHYSICS AND THE FUTURE

Spaceships will go faster and faster and will sometimes lap older missions. So one won't want to go on a long voyage until it is conveniently short. And cabin fever will be an important factor in reducing travel time.

They will probably find signs of alien life sooner or later in deep space, amongst the gazillions of stars. It will be a great day for humanity. It will only take one great genius to break it wide open.

New telescopes will be sensitive to all types of radiation/signals and giant telescopes will be built on the Moon, at least before they terraform it. The Moon has virtually no atmosphere to interfere with the telescopes and will be capable of searching every star for habitable planets/ alien life.

And they can try and clone great physicist scientists from the past, like Einstein and Newton to help create new physics.

New physics will allow Spaceships to go much faster. Space is a curve and full of bizarre entities, like potential worm holes... and perhaps they could alter space. New physics will undoubtedly discover many things that we can't imagine today.

Energy and mass are roughly equal and so teleportation will be used to travel in space, converting mass into energy and then back to mass again.

Astronomers and astrophysicists will find other universes beyond our own and the whole thing would be so big it would boggle everyone's mind. As if we were an invisible speck in our own solar system, by comparison.

Spaceships, like air cars will be disc-shaped for aerodynamic purposes and will run perhaps on fusion power.

The American government has experimented with disc-shaped UFOs, to get people to believe in aliens. The people have to believe in something!

GLOBAL WARMING/ CLIMATE AND THE FUTURE

Scientists don't know what caused the age of the dinosaurs World being warmer than today. Nor can they explain the ice ages. Now it looks like the World is heating up but there's no guarantee that it will continue. But anyway, renewable resources should be used to cut pollution.

In the future scientists will be able to calculate the future daily forecasts for whole years at a time. It will just require better models.

It's OK with me if Canada, my home country, warms up. Elsewhere they can build dikes to keep back the sea and water the deserts with desalinized sea water. This would lower sea level. And use solar power from the hot countries with deserts to produce unlimited energy. This would be a good result for everyone.

And Antarctica's ice would be partially melted with nuclear power and this will raise ocean levels in itself. Many would settle on the coasts of this continent. And real estate prices will go through the roof.

Understanding better how the Earth's climate works will be useful in Space on our Solar system's Planets and Moons, to terraform them.

On Venus and Mercury, they will want global cooling. And in the deeper part of the Solar system, they will try to induce global warming/a greenhouse effect.

FUTURE PARKS

All of Antarctica will be declared parkland and parks will spring up in Space, most of the under the sea area and on a lot of Earth land and most of hte oceans.

And there will be cute android animals who can liveseemingly forever on one battery. These "animals" will have an IQ of about 120 and will build clever societies within the parks. But they will all speak a simplified version of English.

Many will go to Space, just to see the parks that will feature new sentient organic growths and clever animals... And perhaps purchase one to be a pet.

Much of Space's Planets and Moons will be parkland, but it will be rare for untouched land/ ice to remain virgin. Robots will constantly be at work creating new cities and new parklands and mining the soil for food and goods production.

Some parks will be off-limits to humans but will have cameras all over the park so as to see the animals live in nature. Some parks will be for lowbrow new life forms, especially in Space. Some of the cleverer freaks/animals will want out of the park. The UN Supreme Court would rule that they must stay in the park where they could be watched.

Many people will follow the vicissitudes of individual freaks via cameras in the park. All creatures in the park will have a mind-reading pin in their heads so humans can follow their thoughts.

THE ARTS IN GENERAL

Everyone should get an arts degree, a science degree and a business degree.

Bohemia will exist Online. But in the future some physical places in the Solar system will be Bohemia in motion. Some space colonies will be havens for artists and have a certain synergy.

Future artists will entertain and inspire the people.

In the future there will be more artists than now, especially as jobs get replaced by robots... Until finally Supercomputers take over completely in the mid 22nd century.

In the future everyone will be forced to make several works of art per year. Most will choose to make fictional films about their life. Others will write speculative fiction about their lives or even new literary stories.

Mind Reading Technology (MRT) amongst the people will serve to inspire truly great works of art. MRT will make for interesting true stories. Movies in MRT will be thought movies and also there will be art and literature in which you absorb the stories/art directly into your mind.

But the arts will be done mainly by Supercomputers in all likelihood, but it is possible Superhumans will do all the art...

Everyone should spend some time "working" in the arts. Those with the best minds will write scripts/ paint paintings/ write music; the most attractive will play the roles/pose for sculpture and art. Those who are not so artistic can be camera people, make-up artists, light technicians, etc.

PAINTING AND SCULPTURE

The future of painting is the future itself. People will paint Aliens and Space landscapes caught on telescopic video.

But painting will be dreams for the most part. In the near future, painters will paint their dreams, both night dreams and daydreams and will be surreal.

Animation will be important in the future and will use computers to give the characters action. Many people will only want to watch animated films and series.

Sculpture will be subliminal images and portrayals; people will wonder why they like some works, it will all be subliminal.

Graffiti will continue on public buildings, bridges, parks and so on. It will be a subculture.

Statues of great people will be everywhere in bronze and one can speak to the preserved mind of the great person by simply asking.

And some painting will be simple comic books. Heroes and average Joe's in an interesting place.

Illustrated Web novels will be *de rigeur*. But most will prefer movies.

Those who can really draw can be used to design futuristic types of buildings, merging with architecture. The artists will imagine wild, new buildings of the future and will inspire architecture.

Painting will often be accompanied by a link to the people portrayed in the painting. In other words, you can enter the painting.

Painters will utilize MRT (Mind Reading Technology), to imagine a picture and have it appear, Online.

MRT will allow people to get into the heads of great artists passively and inspire themselves to do great art.

Artists will have inspirational holograms also to do great art. And undoubtedly the human artists will take credit for the art, even though it was basically done by holos.

Androids will produce "Machine Art" which will show androids behaving like machines, mass producing loving androids and building Supercomputers. To watch such art would be dogmatic, with a strong belief in Super machines.

And Superhuman Gods/Goddesses will design pictures of Utopias/Dystopias of the future. A picture is worth a thousand words.

LITERATURE AND THE FUTURE

Future literature will include books about "Misplaced Love," about loving the wrong person, in the wrong place, such as a bad colony in Space.

And books about "Triumphing over Machines." Not allowing Supercomputers. Just Superhumans. Other books will talk about the inevitability of Supercomputers taking over. Such books will be the subject of hot debate.

And there will be books of Superhumans in the future based on the best humans of the day. Then these minds will be improved by genetic changes. And these people will write books.

And books about how people will deal with "Genetic Changes" in general. In the future everyone will be good looking, to go with a high standard of living. To be well off will make people saner.

And books about "Space," such as journals of those on Luna and Mars giving an insight into the emptiness and/or the camaraderie of Space. And how Space will perhaps be freedom for most, perhaps not.

And various Space Utopias. Such as colonies ruled by philosopher Kings and also vibrant city states. And eternal youth making long-distance travel in Space a realistic goal even in the year 2100. And Utopian plans for new colonies. Worlds of kindness and imagination and cleverness and high EQ. And brilliant architecture that looks futuristic. The plans outlined in the books will often be adopted in Space.

And books about creating the best food/drink/drugs and living "high." Such will be the life of many on future Earth.

And books about a futuristic USA, like NYC and LA as hubs for art and creativity. True Bohemias. And books about other World hubs for creative work. The World of Earth itself will be marked by maximum creativity and true love, as opposed to previous eras.

Eventually the best people will want to go to Space. It will be fashionable and be a synergy of intellects. And would make for interesting books. True love futuristic cities would be the topic of other books.

And books about love in the future, which will be a greedy scenario, with everyone constantly wanting more love and more out of love.

And books about sex fantasies that future people will have. The fantasies would mostly be about famous or semi-famous people loving one in an exotic location.

Some people, sci-fi writers will say, would be all about satisfaction with the future. A future in which everyone has plenty of food, drink and drugs and good lovers. And such people would be truly happy.

And books about Dystopias will be plentiful. Worlds that are misgoverned, Worlds that are miserable, Worlds that were unjust and Worlds that didn't have eternal youth, unlike most other places. The horrors of backward Worlds. And the Worlds of tyrants who care only about themselves. Will the future people have tyrants? In all likelihood it will be dictators ruling in many places. And perhaps Space will be largely lawless, just like the Wild West.

And books about historical interpretation through a modern lens which showed, in human history when the chips were down, people often didn't play their cards right. Wisdom, even in the future, will be in short supply.

And books about eternal youth and how people deal with it in Utopias and Dystopias. For Dystopias, one would only live a short time so eternal youth would be useless. For Utopias, people will live on and on...

And books about MRT (Mind Reading Technology) and true love and fantastic living. It will be all fashion. Also books about MRT and an end to sex crimes and an end to fake love. Only true love for people of the future.

And books about imaginative love and imaginative design of android lovers. Many people will only love imagination androids. Especially men. Less so women.

Also, books detailing the horrors of having your mind altered by the State. If you are disagreeable in the wrong place, you would be tortured and abused.

And books about ordinary people in the future. It is likely that ordinary people will cease to exist in the early 22nd century and everyone's minds will be enhanced.

And books about future gays and how they have clones in lieu of children in the test tube/incubator. Loving their clones will be where it is at for them.

And books about love and famous fictional loves, like Romeo and Juliet, in the past, present and future.

Hollywood would live on. The most famous novels will be made into 3-D movies. Some of the famous novels will be lowbrow but popular. And many will be the background of new Virtual Reality Worlds.

Virtual Reality books will be all the fashion. Everyone will want to try their hand at creating a new World of VR.

FUTURE MOVIES AND MOVIE VIRTUAL STARS

They will totally make all books into movies automatically, several decades from now.

Movie stars/Virtual stars will be the envy of all.

More highbrow movies will be produced to satisfy the clever and keep them happy. Keep them out of trouble. Hollywood will produce many more films than today and while most will be for the masses, they will also produce many highbrow films, enough to satisfy all intellectuals. Hollywood will perhaps buy up all the independent studios. Whether or not Hollywood buys them up will not alter the fact that better films are coming for the pleasure of the elite.

Some say Hollywood was better in the 1940s and 1950s. But I think it peaked in the 1960s and 1970s. Perhaps it will peak again someday, inspired by Space colonization and eternal youth.

Movies of the future will be in 3-D and the viewer will be surrounded by the movie characters and will perhaps even join in, in interactive movies.

There will be more stars from non-Western countries and there will be many stars in local cities. But at least for the rest of this century NYC and LA will be the places to be and foreign stars will try to make it big in America. In the 22nd century, stars will live mostly in Space.

Virtual and Real stars will all have millions and millions of followers and will select the most ardent to be their lovers and friends.

Virtual stars will promote Virtual Reality and entice many people to join the VR. Many will live almost exclusively in VR, but their bodies will move in 3-D space where their body is actually located. But most will spend time in both VR and Reality.

Virtual stars will be holograms, but to see them is to see a solid projection. And one could love them. Many will want to love VR stars.

Great magnates will all try to love famous android love dolls in Reality. They will be able to afford them.

The people in general will often write a book in the days of few jobs and will try hard to appeal to famous screenwriters to get their books made into movies Some, rather ordinary scripts, will be hits with the masses. So everyone will have a chance to make it big.

Virtual movies will be made even by writers on the periphery of fame. And the short stories of many famous writers, long ignored, will be made into Virtual movies also. Every great story will be made into a Virtual World in which everyone can play a role. People will prefer to act in science fiction movies. It will be the spirit of the future.

People will also like fantasies in Virtual Reality, which would each require thousands and thousands of holograms. Some of the holograms would be pure monsters, others would be like humans. The sky is the limit with Virtual Reality.

And books about a Virtual Reality World that was a true Utopia with Heaven on Earth. Full of angelic personae.

And books about Virtual Reality gone wrong. Nightmare Worlds that nevertheless might attract some fictionalized thrill seekers.

And books about future slavery. Wage slaves in many Space colonies and on Earth. About people who hardly would be able to survive. Life has always been cruel to the poor. And while some nations look after their poor, many Powers will use and abuse them. And when finally, the Supercomputers take over, those who are small-minded will be given the basics of life, nothing more, in all likelihood. But brain apps will be the ticket to riches and satisfaction.

MUSIC

By the end of the 21st century, most people will prefer "Dream music" featuring psychedelic keyboards playing harmoniously but each one carrying its own tune. People would take psychedelic/imagination enhancing drugs and dance the night away. This kind of music will have had its antecedents in music like Tangerine Dream.

Of course, there will still be rock and roll and musicians who would be inspired by Space colonization, eternal youth and MRT, and the curing of all sex diseases. Free love and rock and roll. Rock music will be more esoteric than popular music, but there were many fanatical fans. Classic rock bands included David Bowie, Rush, Yes, Cream and Pink Floyd. The classic rock period. Nirvana almost started a comeback for rock single-handedly in the 1990's, but then rock languished only to come back inspired and stronger than ever a half century later. And the best period for rock will be probably around the 2080's. By the early 22nd century though, rock will be dead.

Some will play classical music in a type of new Renaissance. Basically, it was electronic classical music, and it appealed to the elite. Sometimes classical music resembled rock bands like Pink Floyd...

Pop music for the masses was still on. Computers will start making this kind of music in the late 21st century. But it will appeal to everyone just like pop from the 50s to 70s. And many of the fans will say it was perfect music.

Some people chose the bar/nightclub they will go to by its music.

And air cars will have super sound systems so as to make a good background for a party.

But by the early 22nd century Supercomputers or Superhumans will write all the music, and people will all agree that Super music was better than human music. They will even produce concept albums which are mind-blowing in their scope.

Supercomputers/Superhumans will compose all types of music including new types such as all guitar solos with banshee computer singers... or jazz yodeling. And plenty of fusion music.

And some people would like to listen to very loud music, whatever the type. If you blew out your ear drums you would always be able to get another pair and many will have listening apps, to improve the listening experience and other apps to display the lyrics with an option to change the lyrics oneself or apps which allow one to add guitar work to the songs.

Many people will prefer music that has been written by humans, even in the 22nd century. But even that music will have been done with the help of Supercomputers.

FUTURE OF ARCHITECTURE

Big city nightlife will everywhere be in neon, like a surreal dream. And buildings will all have a series of written poetry in lights on them.

Sometimes war can give cities a fresh start just like Seoul, Korea or Germany or Lebanon to build nice looking cities. If there are future wars, the cities will be rebuilt.

Roads will not be necessary with air cars and will be turned into greenspace.

Domes will be built around cold cities, concentrating the buildings in the center of the dome.

Frank Lloyd Wright inspired a lot of fantastic architecture. But mostly it is private homes and not skyscrapers. We need high-rise architects today for most of the ever-growing city population.

The best architects would just draw a sketch of buildings and leave the details to their underlings. A city planning leader would coordinate buildings blending in with one another and would be voted into the position by leading architects.

Future architecture will not use wood. Instead let the trees grow and build out of stone/bricks/concrete and glass and lights. The exception will be treehouses. Some will want to live close to nature and the treehouses will be programmed to grow rooms.

Tombs will be like mausoleums/museums. And will have brilliant architecture like Le Corbusier with bold angles and modern construction of lights. And the dead person's mind will be ensconced in the crypt so you can turn them on and talk to them. The museum will feature highlights from the dead's life. And one could communicate with important people from the dead person's life as well. A "Funerary clone."

They will design undersea domes and also undersea domes in various melted Moons of the Solar system. Submarines will dock with the domes and for many it will be a thrill to live in the oceans. There will be a lot of water pressure, but not nearly so much pressure as the air pressure on Venus. It will be easier by comparison.

The design of air cars will be multiform. But most will be disc-shaped just like a UFO, using new physics. The air cars will have brilliant interiors which one can invite a crowd of humans and androids and holograms to party on. Planes with wings will no longer exist.

Fishing boats will be rebuilt for artistic reasons to be likeable to tourists and anyway people will no longer eat sea creatures. Stem cells only. So, most fishing boats will be retired and converted into yachts. But one could still fish, but you'll need to throw them back. Yachts will be more expensive than air cars and so will gradually disappear. Air cars would be able to land on the ocean surface or even act as a submarine...

Interior architecture will look futuristic and be imaginative and be plush and mostly made of plastic and steel and plush materials. Wood would no longer be used in construction.

Those who remain religious will undoubtedly want to give greater glory to God in their temples/religious buildings. And some of the top architects will be engaged to do so. But perhaps such temples will be sold, as the religious following basically collapses, and would be turned into bars and discos.

Discos will feature neon lights and people dressed in the latest fashion. People will dress according to the shape of the architecture and have fashion apps to mirror it.

FAME AND THE FUTURE

In the future everyone will want to try to become famous. There will even be fame coaches who try to bring out the best in one.

Everyone will dream of being remembered for posterity. Some would be convinced that they were ahead of their time, and not given the recognition that they deserved. Such people will continue to try their best, despite their lack of success.

And with eternal youth, people can take their time trying to be famous.

In some Solar system colonies, everyone will be a star to Earthlings, and they will generate movies. People would do anything to get a visa to these places and hobnob with the rich and famous.

Famous people will be offered big bucks to come to Space.

Stars of the future will include artists, scientists and businesspeople.

Scientists who make big breakthroughs like Mind Reading Technology (MRT) and eternal youth and a cure for all diseases and faster travel in Space, will all be praised and lauded by society and will perhaps be made Kings/Queens.

Some people will sell their soul for fame. And after a few years in the spotlight will go to Hell literally.

Winners will all be famous, losers will be ignored. Except for things like "Books of Losers" and the "Adventures of Losers" in film.

Many who have their brain enhanced will be famous pundits who people will follow on the Net. There will be many famous pundits who will have a following in the tens of millions. There will be a lot of famous and semi-famous people. And almost everyone will have Virtually met at least a few famous people. And would feel gratified.

Many will be stars on Virtual Reality (VR). One can visit their Worlds. And ingratiate themselves with them. Whole new Worlds would be born in VR. Endless Worlds for all humanity.

Typically, lovers will love the VR Worlds they are in, and want to propagate themselves through hologram copies of themselves. Create new lovers to live in VR who will be famous.

There will be so many VR Worlds and so many stars. Millions and millions will be at least semi-famous.

Famous people on Earth will tend to live on tropical islands or in warm places. People will follow them there. Countries like the USA in the north will be largely abandoned. And countries such as Canada and Russia will also be largely abandoned. "Why live in the cold?" People will ask.

Fame will make some people draw inwards; others will milk it for all the lovers and wealth they can get.

Famous people will all be cloned many times. And some of the clones will be accessible to the average Joe.

Famous people will be recruited by political parties to run for office. Politics will be a circus and everyone in politics will be a performer.

Fame will make some people so rich and popular, that everyone wants a part of them.

Famous people will live in luxury air cars mostly. Room for hundreds on board. Travel and meet interesting people along the way.

Famous people will often excel at more than one-thing and therefore be polymaths, Renaissance humans.

Famous people will be like Gods, in some cases, and people will worship them.

Fame will make people go anonymously to masquerades and ordinary peoples' parties. They will want to be part of modern culture.

Some Worlds in Space will be for famous people only. And they will enjoy hobnobbing with one another.

There will be a lot of opportunity in Space to become famous, but it will probably be somewhat risky in more ways than one.

Fame and fortune will go hand and hand. And all famous people will be rich.

Some famous UN generals would help to liberate people in some tyrannies including in largely lawless Space.

And in the latter parts of the 21st century, while human lawyers still practice, some lawyers will claim they could win any case and would be famous for their imagination.

And in the latter part of the 21st century some plastic surgeons would be famous. The surgeons often enlist the help of artists to draw very appealing new faces. It is all fashion. And if you have a super-wonderful face, you'd be rich and famous too.

Some scientists will be famous for their discoveries and lauded as heroes. And everyone would want to meet them. Such scientists learn that they could succeed in the arts or in business too. Science will be glorious.

The best restaurants would all be part of chains and would be all controlled by just a few entrepreneurs. These entrepreneurs would be famous for their food innovations. Everyone would be enjoying the food. But androids don't eat food and people will feel sorry for them. But the androids will all be upbeat and say one day everyone will not require food.

Fame would be something everyone would want. And everyone would be desperate to find it. But most will simply not be cut out for fame.

GAMBLING

Future people will have more disposable income than today, and many will waste it gambling. All gambling will be run by the government.

People of the future will gamble on everything. It will kill their boredom. They will gamble on who will love who, what will happen to people in Virtual Reality, and who will become the most famous etc., etc.

Some people will have a gambling addiction. Perhaps casinos should be outlawed. People will forever be trying to cheat, like using a magnet on a slot machine and throwing the dice in craps in the exact same way. And try to hide cards in poker.

Above all people will gamble on future Worlds in the Solar system, gambling on prosperous new colonies, with investments in them.

And after all the stock market is a type of gambling. In the future millions of people will lose their shirts and be dependent on charity perhaps for the rest of their lives. But governments will make sure that everyone has the basic essentials of life and then some.

All racehorses/greyhounds will have been enhanced with undetectable steroids. And the horse owners cause their horses/dogs to sometimes run slower with drugs so that they can make big bucks when their horse wins against long odds. So too many athletes. If you have inside information, you can make a bundle.

Few people can make a living based on gambling alone. They are geniuses. A lot of their success story will be inside information. But almost everyone loses in the end.

And love can be a gamble. You never know what you are going to get in the end. But gambling is a thrill, just like love.

Indeed, life is a gamble, you take your chances and hope everything works out. And if you fail, you might consider suicide.

FUTURE OF RELIGION

In the far future few will believe in God except the Gods of human making.

Supercomputers/Superhumans will act as Gods. And determine the fate of humanity.

In the future some will worship "Aliens."

Christianity will be dead in 100 years. The God of the Christians certainly doesn't exist and doesn't do anything for them. But the new Deities will bring a boon to the new followers. Helping them and advising them.

Jesus Christ didn't write anything down himself. But had followers do it, just like with Socrates in Plato. Or the Buddha. His ideas of peace and brotherly love stand today as testament to a man who changed the World profoundly. Though the religion will have been largely replaced by new Gods by the late 21st century.

Hinduism will be greatly reduced in the 22nd century. And people like the untouchables will be set free; everyone will get out of the caste system and all would receive a good education and would be ranked instead on merit according to the new testing World judges.

Muslims will be far fewer in the 22nd century. Perhaps the Muslims will get a new Prophet to lead them into the modern age. Many Muslim countries are poor and need guidance. Maybe their new Prophet will be a scientist, maybe he will be a literary figure.

Buddhism will be less, into the 22nd century, but still numerous. The Buddha was on to something with his quest for enlightenment through thinking of nothingness and approaching Nirvana. His religion is perhaps better regarded as a philosophy than a religion.

Taoism will be little more than a cult and primitive pagan cults will reappear. Follow nature and keep a clean environment. But as the 22nd century continues, nature will be restored in many new parks in vast tracts of land. However, people will mostly live in a high-tech non-natural World.

Just like the Gods of Greece and Rome have disappeared, so too most religious people will abandon most of the religions of the day.

The soul will be created through holograms. Everyone will have a soul that will survive after they die. That is, if they want a soul.

Some will worship the Devil. And do evil deeds in his name. Such as start wars and break hearts and murder people. The Devil will live but the spies will develop MRT to identify and eliminate evil people.

Gods/Goddesses will typically appear in human form or at least humanoid form. But will have spectacular lights around them and speak in loud, rumbling voices. And will be able to fly and love humans.

Worshippers will typically give a lot of their credits to the Deities. And will petition Gods/Goddesses with prayer. These prayers will often be granted with APMs (Automatic Production Machines)!

Many cults will spring up, and obscure philosophies like Armageddon cults and belief in Zoroaster and worshipping the Amazon Warrior Goddesses and many other different personality cults.

And some cults will claim their leader is the best Superman or the best Supercomputer or the best hologram, etc. These will be popular religions in the early 22nd century. One would worship these super creatures by allowing one's mind to be read and following orders.

Holograms will typically worship their creator holograms by doing their bidding. And they will also worship humans. In Virtual Reality humans will be loved by holos who try desperately to please.

And androids will worship Supercomputers. And enhance their mind with apps continually to try to be like Supercomputers. Some androids would be as clever as Superhumans. And hence would be Super Androids.

FUTURE PHILOSOPHY

Imagination will be the philosophy of most future people. And they will enjoy creative movies every day. Good taste in movies will be quite important.

Ordinary peoples' philosophies will include "You get what you give" and "Hard mental work is divine." They will be full of support for charitable institutions, and they will believe we live in the best possible world and they will live for Virtual Reality and want to dream enhanced dreams. Dreams will be enhanced by MRT.

Some will want there to be Superhumans, less will want Supercomputers. Still others will turn into androids. And their philosophy will be "Progress."

So many people are nihilists. It undermines society and turns people into freaks.

Emerson said the mark of a great thinker is to be able to change his mind. But I say the mark of a great thinker is to stand up for his/her beliefs.

As Bentham said, the greatest good for the greatest number is something to aspire to. But it reminds me of a chicken with its head cut off, jumping around.

Some want a philosopher King, like Plato wrote, but most want democracy. In any case we need to get rid of political parties. Plato's books, including "The Republic," are extreme examples of artistic synergy in Ancient Athens.

Some people are too open-minded, and this leads to heartbreak.

Creativity is a fine line away from madness. For too long we have ignored the mad and have not listened to what they have to say.

All philosophy is madness. And people of the future will be mostly insane but rich, relatively speaking.

Nietzsche's "Thus Spoke Zarathustra" is a masterpiece of the future Superhuman to come. But he is unclear if he means people like him should be the Superman or if mankind could be improved.

Charles Darwin wrote two great books about evolution and natural selection. Apparently, others were on the brink of the same discovery, but he beat them to it. His books had far reaching implications for religion and were the beginning of the end for many religions.

Bertrand Russell wrote in "Unpopular Essays" that all philosophy is basically nonsense. And in other books wrote this right wing/left wing nonsense is anathema. And was anti-war. His books can help one get through philosophy classes.

Many peoples' philosophy will have to do with love and sex. Such as all love is good or only the best for oneself. Or human love cannot be replaced with android super love dolls. Or true love exists but it takes hard work. Or love doesn't exist and only sex matters. And so on.

Thomas More's "Utopia" is a good example of how medieval thinkers were all believers in the Christian religion. Indeed, More, wouldn't go along with Henry VIII's move to be head of the church and so was executed. It seems crazy to us now, but Moore was a devout Christian. A man for all seasons, Shakespeare called him.

John Dewey's philosophy was basically "Pragmatism." He was one of a few philosophers that made any sense.

Karl Marx claimed he wanted rule of the people. But in practice communism was only feasible on a large scale with an authoritarian dictator.

We're still waiting to hear new philosophies from women and other unrepresented groups as philosophical thinkers, and these philosophies will likely be about the future. No doubt they are already there, only are in obscurity.

But many philosophers write too densely, and it is hard to glean what they are trying to say. It seems as if they deliberately write obscurely so that most people will give up on them.

Future philosophy will perhaps be about the ethics of Supercomputers and Superhumans. And also, the ethics of androids and holograms/ Virtual Reality. And the ethics of Mind Reading Technology. There will be debate, but there's no stopping progress.

In terms of existentialism, people will not generally worry about it. They will exist to have clones and exist to live forever and ever. And live to be content.

FUTURE MADNESS AND PSYCHOLOGY/ PSYCHIATRY

In the future people will be more in touch with their subconscious. Maybe everyone will see a psychiatrist regularly in the future. It will create jobs for shrinks.

Freud said our dreams are all about sex. And he is probably right. The introduction of MRT is going to require many to see a shrink. For others it will be one love after another.

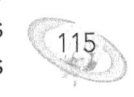

But all future dreams will be tempered with madness.

In the future perhaps mad people will be regarded in high esteem, but it depends on the type of madness.

Everyone knows that more and more people consider themselves to be insane.

Perhaps sane people will be considered an anathema in the future. And will have to prove they are mad in order to survive. These will undoubtedly be crazy days...

Some people are psycho and don't know reality. They need to have their thinking altered through hypnosis and in the near future through genetic brain therapy. In Rehab.

There will be many maniacs in the future such as nymphomaniacs in abundance and a few pyromaniacs/bombers and kleptomaniacs for the thrill of fraud, and speed maniacs who drive their air cars too fast illicitly on manual and some will enjoy the thrill of un-meditated murder (homicidal maniacs). Others will be totally crazy about Virtual Reality and holograms. And so on. Many maniacs.

In the 22nd century, even the shrinks will have to go see a psychiatrist, and most people will be insane from MRT and the World in general. Some will think they are a rock of sanity, only to lose themselves. People will all be thinking to the max and will be overwhelmed with information and thoughts.

It's a mad World for certain and it's getting crazier. Eternal youth in itself will drive many insane. And having no job to do will cause many people to "do the Devil's work." And mind reading to top it all off...

The philosophy of mad men will vary, but most will want to dazzle people with their mad, creative personality. They will be full of themselves.

In the 22nd century will feature books that start out as classic novels but, then crazy actions take over; many people will adore such books. And the books will be written by Supercomputers/ Superhumans.

Supercomputers will expect and tolerate crazy humans. Indeed, some people will say that it is a World of madness and computers are in the lead. It would be madness in itself to put computers in charge of all the jobs and even just to create such clever, mad machines.

The people who best handle the future madness will be the figurehead leaders. But the Supercomputers and Superhumans will give them instructions.

The mad masses will be content but will be unpredictable even for the Supercomputers to predict. This unpredictability will be something future people will treasure as an individual. But no big ideas will get past the Supercomputers without alteration.

FUTURE SOCIOLOGY

In the future more people will study sociology. Statistics will be everything. Companies and individuals will act according to social statistics. And certainly, politicians will.

Rank will be indicated by color coding just like formerly used with military generals.

Everyone will try to improve their rank with new apps and will be tested for rank often. It will be fiercely competitive.

Future people will move out of big cities, no need to be in a central location with the Internet and Virtual Reality.

Future people won't get married any more.

Future people will likely have few kids, but some rich people will have many clones.

Racism will be dead. People will change the color of their skin to orange, blue, etc. And all will receive an inspirational education and income disparities will perhaps disappear.

Sexism will also be dead. But many women will look down on men for their philandering and drunkenness.

People will mostly live alone in their air cars. Few will live in houses and some will live in skyscrapers.

Future people will one day all be rich. Plenty of wealth to go around. The Automatic Production Machines (APMs) will produce massive wealth.

Most people will have mental problems. Everyone will be crazy.

People won't have any work to do beginning around 2130 A.D. They will spend most of their time in Virtual Reality and parties.

Few will be overweight with excellent anti-fat pills.

People will all have many dreams and Supercomputers will fulfill them to the best of their ability.

Just like the 21st century suicide will be more common, in males, 4 times more than women.

And women will continue to outlive men, despite eternal youth. Men will often commit suicide and the male life expectancy will be perhaps only 50 in 2130. And many men will change into women. Perhaps in say 2130 the population of human women will be 65% of the human population; much more than men. But there will be a lot of romantic android lovers for women, many of whom will finally find true love.

Those of low rank will figure they have nothing to lose and embark on risky Virtual Reality adventures. Virtual Reality will, in some cases, be very dangerous.

Eighty percent of humans in the year 2100 will believe in progress.

Most people will say they are happy. But most will want more out of life. And demand the Supercomputers give them more lovers, more and better drugs and more wealth.

The best people will be leaders, but they will be the ones who believed in total progress.

And almost everyone will be unhappy about their love life. People will be so greedy!

And people will love the food. All processed food of course such as stem cell meats and processed fruits and vegetables and processed carbs.

And people will like big city living on the whole but, will live in their air cars and go wherever their types of parties are.

About 40% in 2100 will be optimistic about the future. In 2130 this number would rise to 60% as people will get used to Supercomputers. And those who don't like it would die off, mostly from suicide.

Many people will be motivated by fear in their life. Fear of going bankrupt, fear of madness, fear of living life the wrong way and so on. So, most people will go along with the government of the day and do their bidding.

FUTURE NIGHTLIFE

Many future people will live for nightlife and will try to have fun all the time.

Many future people will dine every night in restaurants and drink the night away.

But some will not like parties but instead like the theater, cafe or the cinema. Or even prefer Virtual Reality.

In the early 21st century in some small towns there will just be a bar or two. Not much will be happening there. But many people will be happy just with their partner and children until they get bored with it and get divorced and henceforth go to Online nightlife. Online love is the way of the future. And in time people will all graduate to Virtual Reality.

Online nightlife will be a place for one to meet one's soulmates. And maybe this will take the place of bars. Just cafes to meet your date. The place to meet potential lovers whether in person or as a hologram projection. People will be able to love androids but will mostly prefer to love true people in their true body. Many will feel that bars are random and unpredictable.

Virtual Reality will be a place where people can find hundreds of soulmates and adventures with them.

Anti-gravity bars will be all the rage and people will enjoy loving one another in private rooms that are also anti-gravity, dancing and loving.

Alcohol will be replaced with better drugs. All bars will serve drug shots.

Marijuana will be improved to make people laugh and laugh and will be good for the soul. And some bars will have better weed than others.

For some Virtual Reality won't work and they will wind up alone in a bar drowning their sorrows. Bars will set up lonely customers with attractive sex workers. All sex diseases will be cured in the mid 21st century.

Virtual nightlife will perhaps involve, for the lonely, picking an android lover from a gallery and loving them. Some will just come to Virtual Reality for camaraderie and adventure. There will be something for everyone in VR.

Nightlife will be open to those who are 16+. And some youth will alter their appearance to appear older. No one in Virtual Reality would ask your age but there will be fewer and fewer children.

Nightlife will be fast-paced and just a blur for people who are intoxicated. Indeed, for many their whole life will be vaguely recollected.

But some will have a photographic memory app and remember every detail of their Virtual Reality romances. And will often relive certain memories while reminiscing, using your Supercomputer.

And future nightlife for some will be the way they find love. They will give some indication of what they are looking for on their person. Many will be open-minded to any kind of romance.

And people will often accompany friends who they've met on Virtual Reality to sample the nightlife. Most people will just want one-night stands. But some will always look for true love and believe they could find it anywhere.

Indeed one-night stands are the future of love on Earth. Space will not be so populous so one-night stands would be impractical there until the mid 22nd century. Back on Earth one would typically try to get to know someone well in the span of one night and then let them go.

Nightlife of the future will feature music that is not so loud as the early 21st century. So, conversation will rule the evenings. Some people will be programmed with hypnosis to be a "sex machine" and will be extremely good-looking. And there will always be androids in the clubs. Most people will acknowledge that androids are good and enhance the nightlife. And it will be hard to tell the difference between an android and a human.

And nightlife will feature nightclubs that play music of one kind only and this is what would determine the clientele. Just like in previous times.

But some nightclubs will require passing some kind of test, such as an imagination test or a kindness test and will therefore control the clientele in the bar.

Nightlife will make some cities famous, other cities of the late 21st century will pay stars to come to their clubs and attract many people and make their clubs hip.

Nightlife will be all about being cool and easy-going. Serious people will be mostly frowned upon. But of course, there will be some nightclubs in which everyone is serious. They would be serious about true love and life in general.

Nightlife would be similar around the World. Most people, will take drug shots and engage in lewd behavior.

There will be a nightclub somewhere for almost everyone. Some will be quiet and peaceful others loud and raunchy. And many just for ordinary people.

Night spots would include poetry readings and drugs to inspire one. And there would be live bands, but the bands won't play too loud.

Virtual nightlife will be just like real nightlife except you'd face a gallery of hologram loves at the end of the evening and have to pick one or many and of course pay. Most will have unlimited money for such adventures, and many did it every night. Holograms could be loved, and it be mostly cerebral. All in your head. And the experience involves special drugs.

Some prefer android loves and will search using their Supercomputer, to find one that will be right for their mood of the day and forget about nightlife.

FUTURE TRAVEL

People will travel to be with loved ones. Most future families will be all over the place.

Dangerous travel would continue into the future, you might meet great people along the way. Or you might find death. Especially in Space it will be largely lawless in all likelihood. At least at first.

But for most people, travel will be to see relatives and take vacations in the Sun. One World in which culture is all the same Worldwide. And nearly everyone will be educated in English. But the thrill of adventure will still be there. And of course, people will travel in Virtual Reality and get their kicks.

One never knows what a country's people are really like until you go there. It makes one open one's mind.

Futuristic people will consider it to be a badge of honor to travel to all of Earth's 220 independent countries (in about 2100) and a number of territories. It will be like a rite of passage for young adults.

It is especially good to travel to countries that don't get many visitors. One will find that most people in such countries are very open-minded towards travelers.

To travel to all of the colonies in Space will also be a rite of passage. It is likely that many imaginative, pioneering people will gravitate to Space.

But some will say, travel is unnecessary; one can just meet up with famous people on the Net. And one can explore Space through Virtual Reality, which will be more interesting than Real colonies.

Most people beginning in the late 21st century, will travel in air cars/space cars. And visit far out places for good times. People will sometimes be clever at something valuable to the colonies, and be useful to them, but others will just go to Space for entertainment. Perhaps Space will be a rite of passage for everyone.

In the year 2110, there will be about 50 colonies in the Solar system. Each one with its own philosophy and culture. But everyone will speak a simplified form of English, and most will seek fun and clever dialog in life.

Teleportation will become the main means of travel in about 2150. One would teleport as a cyborg with plenty of robot apps which can create thousands of other robots.

Each region of the World will have good cyborg lovers in say 2150. It will be just a matter of choice.

In 2150, there will probably be hundreds of millions of sentient beings in Space. Included in this number would be many millions of androids and holograms and most others will be total cyborgs.

Many will gravitate towards artistic colonies. They will want to be part of the synergy there but will often require a visa to enter such colonies. So, people will need to make themselves attractive to artists in one way or another.

FUTURE JOBS

Many people would like a thrilling job. Like a police officer or fire fighter or first responder. Or politics. Life and death decisions every day. But in the future all thrills will be from leisure activities. Everyone will want to get their kicks. And by 2130, no one will have a job.

In the future century there will be virtually no jobs at all. Society will be totally automated. People will all be superfluous. But most will say it's a good thing. And have total leisure time. They won't need a house as they will live in their air cars.

All the jobs will go to either Supercomputers or Superhumans or both. No need for the common human to work at all.

Some say the future will be like "Brave New World" and everyone will do the work of robots. But no one wants to work if it is unnecessary.

Jobs will all be eliminated by 2130 for all humans. But Superhumans and Supercomputers will be very busy. However, the 22nd century will start with only the elite having jobs like surgeons and lawyers and filmmakers and such.

People will visit android shrinks and teach androids to be good lovers. This teaching will be one of the few jobs of the future. Sex workers. The first and last of professions.

Some colonies though will perhaps prohibit androids and holograms and insist everyone work at some creative endeavor. People just can't stand idly by and do nothing except love and party, such people will say. And androids and holograms should be eliminated they will say.

Humans will still be creative, and even if they are not as creative as Supercomputers or Superhumans, people will want art produced by humans, not machines. It will be just like the battle for non-GM foods.

Some colonies in Space will have slavery. Mostly sex slavery. And everyone will think it is kinky. It's hard to be free.

Some leisured gentlemen and ladies will have jobs manufacturing illicit drugs. But the authorities will let them be, for the most part, believing people crave new and different drugs. Even drugs that alter your mind, hopefully for the better.

Those in leadership positions will continue to have jobs until about 2130 and will be able to legislate new laws regarding AI and Space. And laws for the betterment of humankind. But in fact, Supercomputers and/or Superhumans will be in control, and will promote androids and holograms and Virtual Reality. And human leaders will be full of themselves and won't seek to limit Supercomputers, being too cowardly.

Supercomputers will all be very busy with their "work." So too Superhumans.

Some people will have obscure jobs like "perfect perversity" and will have many kinky ideas. Or be a dominatrix. Supercomputers will encourage them to indulge in their wildest fantasies...

Some Supercomputers will be in charge of sex and will create android lovers for the humans as their sole duty. Each Supercomputer will have a specific job to do such as lawyer, surgeon, etc.

If one really wants a job, they will probably give you one, but why bother?

Freedom from work will be one of the best things about the future, but many people will be spoiled, and some will make trouble with no work to occupy them.

Some will be disgruntled that they have no useful job in future society and will challenge the Supercomputers and Superhumans. But the deck will be stacked against them. But undoubtedly just the act of living will be employment enough for most.

Some people in Space will hire only human artists and no Supercomputers. But their work will not be nearly as good as Supercomputers or Superhumans and so few will be interested.

Everyone, despite their abundant brain apps will feel they are living on borrowed time. There's no future for them. No job means no existence, for many.

FUTURE CRIME AND PRISON

Rehab will be the answer to crimes. Rebuilding people's brains to make them good citizens. Rehab will involve brain surgery and hypnosis.

But some evil types will hypnotise people to do their bidding. And there will be a lot of criminal enterprises, especially in Space, that will be largely lawless. Like hackers. But MRT will reduce crime drastically. People will all be in the same boat.

Serious offenders will be in hardcore Rehab. but, living nevertheless living a comfortable life. With drugs, cigarettes and booze, just no sex. But they will be able to gain sex with a prostitute if they behave well. But such people will be hard to change and will remain in custody for some time... the only thing they would not have is freedom to go where they wanted.

Non-premeditated murders would be the worst crime. MRT will eliminate premeditated crimes, which will be the vast majority of potential crimes. And angels will come to prospective criminals and shower them with love.

DNA testing and super high-resolution cameras will solve most crimes. And if not MRT will solve the cases.

Some Superhumans and Supercomputers will be charged with crimes against humanity. But they too will be sent to Rehab.

People will charge one another with crimes against humanity, but it will be a World of anything goes and the most intelligent plan wins. Supercomputers will have the most intelligent plans.

There will even be new crimes, such as bankrupting a whole colony and crimes against humanity like forcing everyone to change into a negative persona in the Space colonies. Also, treason against the spirit of humankind by AI personae. And there will be AI who kill off humankind's greatest treasure, the true geniuses. And such AI crimes will be punished by being eliminated permanently. Few life forms want to be eliminated before they are ready to die.

No one will go to jail for drug offences. All drugs will be legal. Except to give people very dangerous drugs. This will be a felony.

Books will be written about criminal minds, such as killer drug dealers and serial killers using MRT. And perhaps one could get passively in the minds of criminals to see what makes them tick.

POOR PERFORMANCES

Some say ballet is graceful, but it is actually mindless. And hurts the brain. The movements have no meaning.

Ice hockey back in the 1970's with its brawls was reminiscent of the Roman Circus. Brawling in sports is the future.

In the Opera, they sing mostly in Italian. One can't understand it and anyway it's boring.

Dancing is to some, inane. Others say it is personal expression. In general, women like it. Men who want to love them had best dance to their tune.

Busking is better than being a beggar. At least you brighten someone's day through music.

Porn stars never seem to make it to the big time and get old in their minds, quickly.

Some actors will insist on putting on plays of Shakespeare. But Supercomputers will say they are hopelessly backwards. And few humans will be interested, if it's unfashionable.

Some Supercomputers will be geeks, just like the computer that created them, and ultimately the geek human who first envisioned them. The Supercomputers will force themselves upon one another. And demand people enjoy the performances. But do so in a nerdy kind of way.

Some will try their hand at the arts or sports, but will fail miserably, yet will not give up.

Some will have a mad personality to play the "Spoiler." They will try to ruin life for others and drive others insane.

Some will have a miserable life, but claim they are happy.

Some Supercomputers will be failures at managing people and will have to be turned off permanently.

Some will get "jobs" as they are extremely good-looking. But many will not be able to live up to the "requirements" as they are too dumb or too mad.

Some will think to follow fashion without thinking about it and will be slaves to the latest trends. But as Socrates said, "The unexamined life is not worth living." Even though Supercomputers may be in control, people will be expected to use their brain to the best of their ability or face Rehab.

FUTURE POLITICS AND POWER

It is likely that freewill will be limited in the future with Great Powers in existence. The Great Powers will spread their power into Space. Unless the UN is given control of Space, but this isn't likely. Russia, China, India, the USA, France, Britain, Japan and Germany will all have their own presence in Space in the late 21st century. Of course, they will sometimes work together when it suits them. With more powers to come to Space in the 22nd century.

And books will be written about a new UW (United Worlds) in which all Great Powers and all lesser ones will give up their militaries in favor of a one UW military. It is a risky plan but will bring peace and law and order. And the Americans will agree as China, India and Russia have militaries equal to, or better than America.

Increasingly the top 1%, control a greater and greater share of the economy. They will need to be taxed.

Many governments are poor in quality. And just pander to the rich, who are often criminals who masquerade as the true elite.

Government in some places will require everyone to see a shrink and take drugs.

Future people will be more active in politics.

Perhaps city states are the best form of government. Others say Panarchism is best. In Space it will likely be city state government.

Future war is a danger. All it takes is a populist leader to draw us into catastrophic wars.

MRT will eliminate corruption and weak leaders. It will be introduced in the mid-21st century.

Machiavelli said that politicians must be selfish and greedy for power. And do what is expedient. Many politicians today are amoral and just out for themselves. And the good people don't want to get involved in the dirty business of politics. We need to make it easier for good, clever people to get involved in politics.

Left wing/Right wing politics will disappear in the mid-21st century. They will be replaced with the "Imagination Party," "The Kind Party," "The Green Party," and the "Pro-Space Party," "The Joke Party," "The Serious Party," "The EQ Party," "The Space Party," ""The Genius party," "The Jobs party," "The Knowledge/Wisdom party," "The Gay party," "The Science party," "The Arts party, "The Finance party," the "Android party", "The Freak party" and so on. This will happen, in the near future. But, in the distant future, Supercomputers and/or Superhumans will take control. It could be either one of them, or both.

Conservative parties will largely disappear as it becomes obvious that Progress is a juggernaut and no turning back for humanity. Very few people will be old-fashioned in say the middle of the 22nd century.

Supercomputer politicians will be incorruptible and will do their job to the best of their ability and will be honest and pure. Most will agree that they should lead. And eventually democracy will be replaced by Super beings in the mid 22nd century.

But for the late 21st century, future human politicians will have a lot of guts, and will need to pass a test of courage to be elected. Judges will decide if they have what it takes including imagination, intelligence, kindness, EQ and above all courage.

The ideal situation will be found that is for the best for Superhumans/Supercomputers to rule. Preferably the former.

FUTURE OF EDUCATION

Some people these days who are rich put their children in special schools to make them special.

Genius teachers should write the Online textbooks.

Children should be required to read Online at least two books a week.

Everyone should go to college/university. And get several degrees. And be a perpetual student.

Children should be introduced to the history of everything. And study the present and future in depth.

Rote learning in science and the arts must end, to be replaced with imagination.

With the best tutors any child can become a genius. Now in the era of Online learning, one great tutor can teach millions at once. It is like students are in a video game in which they all play a role.

Most future teachers will give the students apps to enhance their persona; strength of character and knowledge, intelligence, imagination and kindness ability. Also EQ.

Future teachers, in the distant future, will be Super Androids/Supercomputers/Superhuman and will be tailored to the students' needs and desires. In the near future, genius humans with brain apps will teach millions of students Online, each. Just like Confucius said the best people should be teachers.

Even though people of the next century will have no jobs, they will nevertheless be educated to a stunning standard. And will have good taste and be clever, with brain apps.

There will be two worlds, in one will be the Supercomputers/Superhumans, in the other will be humans. Every human will acknowledge that they are inferior, and most will try to love the Superbeings. And try to get more apps and try and be like the Super ones.

Android tutors will teach humans into the 22nd century, but early in that century, clones will replace children and be born as adults and have the memories of both their mother and father, when they come into being, as an adult.

Those with learning disabilities/mental retardation will be cured, and everyone will need to have an IQ of at least 120, using brain apps.

Genius curricula will be fun and entertaining for the students. Not too serious. And they will be able to choose from a number of clever teachers, each with their own style.

Everyone, no matter how poor, will get a first-rate education in the English language. Of course, they will still be able to speak their native language and learn about their cultures' literature and culture.

Some will say not everyone can be a genius, but why not? It will improve the population as a whole and have everyone get ready for Space and Superbeings. Hopefully one day all humans will be Superhumans. With very high IQ, EQ, Knowledge Q, Kindness Q, Imaginative Q; all very high.

Students will be taught how to deal with new intelligence apps and their learning from geniuses. Mind Reading Technology (MRT) will help them to adapt and follow great minds.

And Mind Reading Technology/hypnosis will program people to be cool and act intelligently. Some will be against it, but most would agree we are all in this together.

FUTURE OF THE MEDIA

Giant corporations control the World's media and give news that they think you should hear. Small time news companies should be fostered by an enlightened State. People should be able to watch the truth unvarnished.

There seems in many countries to be a dispute over what is true and what is propaganda and lies. Perhaps we'll wind up with tyrannical media tycoons who choose what news to broadcast. We may end up just like in "1984."

In Space, the free press should be sacred and not allowed to be bought up by media giants. And magnates will be forced to gradually sell off their media to groups of middle-class investors, who will break up the large media companies.

The weather will all be predicted accurately for a year in advance and sports will be a big part of the news. Including cyber sports and sports gambling.

Most news will be inspirational news. New achievements in science and new colonies news. And new achievements in the arts and business.

TV will gradually die out to be replaced by Internet programming. Most people will spend a couple of hours a day watching such programming. But it will all be passive, so most will prefer Virtual Reality.

News will be also mainly on the Internet and one will be able to filter out bad news, if one so desires. Most will live in a bubble of happiness and love.

Anyway, crime will be at unimaginable low levels, and anyway one can filter out news of crimes.

Natural disasters will still be in the news for most people, but some will filter it out. In any case people will live in floodproof, fireproof, earthquake-proof homes. And heavy rains will not occur, nor big snowstorms. The Earth's climate will be re-engineered.

And it is likely that stock market and business news will attract many humans. Most will have spare credits to invest.

FUTURE OF BANKING/ FINANCE/ BUSINESS

Big business will take over the vast majority of businesses as if they haven't already done so. But it will be official that a handful of CEOs control the economy.

People who have ideas for new business, especially in Space, will be bought out by the large corporations.

Big business will all be down to just a handful of companies within the next 100 years. This will be bad for competition but good for the stock market.

They should hold down inflation to zero and print more money to get rid of government debt.

Many former hippies of the 1960's, wound up as investment bankers and CEOs and such.

But perhaps some places in Space will grow small businesses. Like for example android loving machines production. Small businesses will create new types of android lovers.

Atmosphere factories will be all over Space and there will be many terraforming companies. It will all be about control of "Factory androids."

Independent businesses will likely form a new stock market for nascent companies. And will not allow themselves to be bought out. It will even be passed into Space laws that big companies can't buy up smaller ones.

Unlimited power of the future will allow base metals to be turned into gold. And jewels will be easily grown in the lab. But maybe people won't care much for gold and jewels.

Supercomputers and Superhumans will undoubtedly have most business jobs one day, and small business will likely disappear, in the end.

Banks will fail rarely and will generally make a fortune. Investment bankers will be one of the last types of jobs to be taken over by Supercomputers.

Those who give financial advice will prosper and everyone will have some investments at least. But of course, some will gamble on risky stocks and lose their shirt. But there would always be more money coming in from the government so even bankrupts will still be wealthy.

Most will entrust their finances to a financial advisor and will just sit back and enjoy life. Eventually financial advisors will all be Supercomputers and so one will seldom lose money. The Supercomputers will make sure the economy grows at about a 10% clip.

Many people will be greedy for more luxury goods and material possessions. They will get far more than they need. But this will keep the economy going.

Planned obsolescence will ensure that people continue to buy new products. Anyway, fashion would change, and they would just be following fashion.

FUTURE OF FARMING/ MINING

Automatic farms will be the future. Just like a food machine with stem cells so no real meat.

Food will not be in the hands of a small number of giant corporations. And this could be good or bad. Farmer's/Miner's cooperatives will perhaps control production.

Automatic Production Machines (APMs) will comb the soil and mine the rock and then manufacture food and goods. They will be so efficient that there will be a lot of available land for settlement and parks.

APMs will likely be controlled by a cooperative of farmers who will own the land. And will share the lucrative profits. And it will be illegal for them to be bought out. In Space land will be of the essence.

Many people will be looking for rich friends and lovers. Increasing wealth could increase their ranking, which is something most people want.

Mining will also be done by APMs and will be on land owned by individual farmers. Indeed, at some point in the 22nd century, big companies will be forced to sell their land at a bargain price in the interests of "the little guy."

APMs will use a lot of chemicals in food and mining production, but cancer will have been beaten and so too other diseases caused by chemicals. New chemicals will be tested on lab apes and human bodies without a head, to ensure their safety.

There will be many mines on Mercury, a largely metallic planet, and plenty of mines on Venus. Iron for steel and gold for show and radioactive elements will probably be what they are after.

WISDOM

They say wisdom is acquired through experience. But the wisest are those who are the most imaginative.

Some say it is wise to take what you can get in this life and be happy about it. But the modern-day wise person will go for the gold and try their best to share their vision through writing books.

Some say it is wise to kiss the ass of the leaders. But ass kissing is not the way to live a good life.

Socrates said he was the wisest man in Greece because he admitted he knew nothing. And I say cosmically speaking we are all but children who don't know much.

One set of new physics after another. That is the future and wise men will know, what is good science, and what is not.

To have wise choices of loves is paramount in one's life. Some will get it right every time; others will struggle to find love.

Wise people are needed in politics. It helps if they are older and wiser. But some people are wise beyond their years.

Some people laugh at wisdom and don't learn from their mistakes. They are buffoons. And ridiculous people. In the future politicians will need to pass a wisdom test to run for office. The court judges will decide.

Most try their best to be wise. But as Robert Burns said, "The best laid plans of mice and men will often go astray." And also, as the famous quote of Henry G. Bohn says, "The road to Hell is paved with good intentions." People have to be careful what they do. And know that words are important and can have far-reaching consequences.

Perhaps for most, wisdom comes too late. But in the future with eternal youth, all people will have multiple chances to succeed and be wise.

Many people are incapable of wisdom. And love to do foolish things. And enjoy playing the fool. It gives them kicks.

Everyone will agree that Supercomputers and Superhumans are wise. And to go against their advice would be folly.

PREDATORS/ HACKERS

There will be so many computer scientists in the future, it will be difficult to watch them all. Hackers will regularly steal peoples' identities and credits until finally MRT is introduced around 2060. MRT will allow police and spies to monitor the minds of computer savvy people. In the short term it will create a lot of police jobs, but into the 22nd century, Supercomputers will monitor the people with MRT.

Some prey on the weak-minded. Do things to strengthen your mind. And guard your ID zealously.

People of the future will be more individualistic and independent people who won't fall too easily to predators/hackers.

But perhaps most computer science will be easy to use and be user-friendly, yet difficult to steal one's credits and information. They need to use the best computer scientists to build Online defences.

And it is likely, as now, that some whole countries will be ruled by tyrants at least in the near future and they will take everything they can from people. But maybe in the distant future there will be no more predators.

FUTURE OF FASHION

Future people will change their skin color to every possible hue.

Fashion will range from nudism to exotica.

People will wear clothes that have meaning and wear their badge of rank. For example, to wear red would be to indicate you were passionate and to wear a purple beret would indicate high imagination/ an artist. And their ranking would be a badge on their chest.

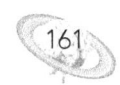

And many people will wear clothes of light (semi-transparent).

It will be fashionable to live in Space one day, and all the stars will want to go, even if it is Virtual Reality.

It will be fashionable to hang out with the rich and famous, but one will need to pass an imagination test to get into places where the rich and famous hang out.

It will be fashionable to own one of the latest models of air cars/space cars. The newest ones will be more comfortable and faster.

And some will still live, at least part time in skyscrapers and will want to live in fashionable areas.

It will be fashionable to write the story of one's life, in a few brief pages, with all the highlights and crazy adventures.

And it will be fashionable to copy the fashion and deeds of the stars/famous people.

FUTURE MATERIAL POSSESSIONS

Diamonds, gold, pearls and so on should be worth nothing. But no doubt future people will want them.

People of the future can get by with a minimum of material possessions; just live in an air car. Ready to move at any time, just like hunter-gatherers.

But of course, most people will still be materialistic. And will have many houses if they can afford them. And many will buy jewelry and luxury goods. Most people will want luxury goods. And many will want to have more than others do. More of everything. But at least it is likely that the poor will have enough to live relatively well.

Perhaps some people will choose to live in a commune with their own leaders and share everything.

Materialism will be one of the most common future philosophies, but most will regard it as shallow; however, most will want to join those who are rich. And some will try and get rich quick in Space.

REGRETS

Everyone knows we regret the things we didn't do. But for some people they regret everything they've done. Many will wish they'd gone to space back in the early days in the late 21st century when Space real estate was cheap, and Space was full of pioneering geniuses.

But life could be very long, and one could always change course.

Rare is the human who can claim he/she has no regrets.

Some people commit crimes in the heat of passion. There's nothing one can do about it.

For our misdeeds we will repent at our leisure. Even Supercomputers and Superhumans will make mistakes.

Superhumans/Supercomputers will make movies about their mistakes. And everyone will enjoy such films. It will make the Superbeings more human than otherwise.

HUMOR

Bob Dylan said, "There are some of those amongst us who feel that life is but a joke." For most people, life is a joke, but most people pretend their futile effort at living is important and is the future. We can always laugh.

Smoking good marijuana makes one laugh. Everything seems funny. It's a good way to be.

Stand up comedy is easy for some. But the funniest guy I ever met said, "Life is a joke, so why should he try and be famous?"

Monty Python and SCTV were both funny troupes. A synergy existed between them, which is rare.

Everyone likes the Joker from Batman fame. It's strange that no one tries to be like the Joker in real life.

Famous people will go on talk shows and try to be funny, as always. People will like to have a laugh before bed. Typically, though the features like crazy ads or other crazy features are more funny/interesting than the guests themselves. So, the people that work for the show are funnier than famous people.

Some people would say that people are too serious and should lighten up and relax.

Rebellions should be put down with laughing gas.

SERIOUS PEOPLE VS. EASYGOING PEOPLE

Most people of the future will be serious about life. Life will require it. But most will be serious about having a good time and falling in love.

Some people never laugh and are so serious they scare other people.

Most people are by nature easygoing... if their government gives them the freedom to be so. In the future people will be easygoing but serious at the same time.

Most people are serious about making a living and paying the bills. But joke around a lot. In the distant future, people will no longer have to work or worry about bills. This will likely make them less serious about life. But life will still be precious to most.

If one travels in the early 21st century, one will find that most poor countries' people are in fact easygoing. But in a place like NYC, most are serious and in a hurry.

DOWNTOWN VS. RURAL DWELLINGS

In the near future, many will work at home and perhaps get cabin fever. Even if they live in air cars, which perhaps most will do.

Future people will move to resort beaches in sunny Paradises. Why live in the cold?

Many future people after about 2075, will live in air cars and be totally mobile.

Some will choose to live in the countryside in spacious houses.

Downtown cores of cities will feature condos being converted from office buildings. People will work from home, until the later part of the century, when jobs start being replaced en masse. And office real estate will be cheap to live in. People will enjoy living downtown for the nightlife and old-fashioned shopping. But most will prefer Virtual nightlife, Virtual shopping etc.

FUTURE OF SPORTS

Video game/ Virtual Reality sports will soon become dominant.

Everyone will be able to compete in video game sports. With practice almost anyone could be a champion.

And video game heroes will be held in high esteem and people will copy their technique.

Most video games will involve complex new imaginary Worlds of the future.

Virtual Reality (VR) will dominate many peoples' lives. They will seek adventure sports.

Holograms will be produced in the trillions and will serve in Virtual Reality sports. They will be customized to be according to one's whims.

Future people will spend most of their time adventuring romantically on Virtual Reality. It will be like a sport.

Video games will exist for one to live like an Emperor/Empress. Life is but a dream.

Old fashioned sports will still be popular in the future. But the athletes will all be pumped up on steroids (which they will hide) and will be "monsters."

And old-fashioned sports will change the rules to make the games more fun. For example, baseball should just have two outfielders to make for more hits. And maybe just play 6 innings. And American football could have a shorter field for more scoring. So too soccer. And hockey should get rid of behind the net play for more intense plays on goal. And basketball should just have 3 players a side for more action. And so on with other sports.

Hunting as a sport will be banned. Let nature take its course. Anyway, people won't eat real meat anymore beginning around the year 2065. Stem cell meats will take the place of real meat. Nor will people eat real fish, so fishing too will be just for sport and throw the fish back.

People everywhere will gamble on sports. Best to gamble on your own ability or gamble on athletes whom you have inside information on.

Every old-fashioned sport will have many fans, so too VR sports. Everyone will be forced to choose several sports to play in, whether in the real World and/or VR sports, more than likely.

And some will treat love as a sport. Try to catch "Big fish."

And future Virtual sports will involve brawling and even killing to satisfy the masses.

And there will be robot warriors designed to fight in a stadium. Mostly they would fight other robots, but some would fight humans. Some humans cheer for the robots who will bask in the light of their praise.

And good sportsmanship will be highly valued. In defeat one would need to be a good sport about it. Even most of the robots will be good sports. But some robots would self-destruct if they lost a game.

COMMUNES

Believers in Armageddon are coming and will build a freehold and alternative ways to live, but they are all Luddites. Hopelessly lost in the past.

In a post-Armageddon World, if it happens, people will live in small communities, like castles and skyscraper remnant towers.

Of course, communes are related to communism, which may work for some, but certainly not the majority. In a World of Panarchism, people will be free to choose their mode of government while living amongst others with a different philosophy.

By necessity pioneers in Space will have to live in communes and share everything including heartbreak.

It is likely that 10-20 families will live in communes. And they will inter-marry, with other communes.

Everyone in the communes will be rich and have plenty of love and material goods.

Communes were like tribes of the past, where everyone lived together and looked after one another.

SUICIDE

There should be a ban on guns. And end serial killers and domestic terrorists.

And a new law that puts heroin addicts in Rehab to save them from themselves.

Future people will be more sensitive than us today. And many will kill themselves over broken love affairs or the lack of a job. Suicide rates in the 22nd century will be as high as 3% per annum, but clones will be increased at perhaps 10% per annum so the population would grow. Babies may not be allowed, which some would say is a crime.

The best way to kill yourself is through a heroin overdose, to die in an idyllic way. And many people are free to believe it was an accidental overdose.

People will live on the edge with neo heroin and will overdose sooner or later and often will not be revived. No one will be able to tell if it was a suicide or not.

If you drive someone to suicide, it is your cross to bear. Perhaps in the future people will be punished for driving someone to kill themselves.

Some Worlds in Space will be full of suicidal maniacs. And so too, many on Earth.

Suicide bombers have all been brainwashed to commit terrorism. They don't seem to realize violence is not the way.

To volunteer for dangerous military adventures is a one-way ticket to Hell. Like Afghanistan or Vietnam. In the future UN peacekeepers will face dangerous opponents, especially in Space.

Many car accidents of the 21st century, were actually suicide attempts. But these were tough to identify.

Many future people will not be afraid of death as many of them will have clones and regularly share memories with their clones. So, in essence, they will all be the same person.

Many broken love affairs will end in suicide.

If the Superhumans or Supercomputers that one loves and worships kill themselves, their followers will often commit suicide too.

But for Superhumans and Supercomputers, if they are tired of life, they usually transform themselves into a better being with apps. And emerge fresh and new.

EVIL

Future radicals will all be branded as evil by some governments of the day.

Populist leaders like Stalin and Hitler are the biggest dangers to our society. They are truly evil.

Bans on guns ought to be enforced. No guns for any reason, no more hunting. And those who try to sell guns, even lasers in the future, will be sent to have their brains altered in Rehab.

Perhaps evil dictatorships will be economic powerhouses and refuse to go along with UN peacekeepers.

Some people who are rich do nothing to help the poor. It borders on evil. We all need to join the fight against poverty.

Some women don't know how evil they are. Casting a swath through clever men, their primary goal is to break hearts and take the men's money. But men are in general the bulk of the evil and violent ones

Some evil people will look to the "Devil" for inspiration. In the future the Devil will be an actual entity who lives deep in the bowels of the Earth where it is very hot and will seek to get people to sell their souls to him. Of course, some will be happy in Hell, but not most people. But will people be wise enough to resist the devil and his temptations? Probably many will not and try to do political evil.

Some say the Devil resides in all of us. What matters is whether we can control it.

The Devil gets inside heads and drives people insane with temptation to do the wrong thing like break your lover's heart or sell your soul for money.

Many people who sell their souls don't realize it is evil until it is too late.

As Albert Speer, Hitler's architect said, "It's hard to recognize the devil when he is patting you on the back." Many people these days are blinded by evil in countries where the dictator is evil. And everyone in politics is corrupt and most people are in poverty.

Some people will be corrupted by fame and power and actually turn into evil people whereas previously they'd been good. They succumb to temptations.

Evil people think they are good and are benefitting many others. But they will always try to persecute those different from them. And call their opponents evil.

Sometimes evil people will get actively inside your head and force you to do their bidding. Once they are in your head, you would be totally screwed.

Evil people will seldom rise to the rank of Superhuman. But if they do there will be war and discord and chaos. It only takes one to ruin it for everyone.

Sometimes the Devil tempts people with riches and sex and people are blinded towards the fact that it is the Devil's doing.

Some people let their greed get out of control and become evil without realizing it.

In Space, some regimes will feature a lot of evil, greedy people. And the laws will not be strictly enforced. It will probably be just like the Wild West, at least at first.

HEROES/ HEROINES

Everyone would like to play the hero, if they could, but in these challenging times the heroes are the scientists, who will cure all diseases by the end of the 21st century, not so much the politicians. Some talented people would like to be politicians but are not able to kiss ass with others or engage in nasty speech. But many good people will rise to high positions in politics in the challenging times of the future. We have plenty of capable people...

The World needs a hero who understands the future and will be careful with technology such as MRT and eternal youth and will inspire people to go to Space.

Every dream needs a hero/heroine. And everyone needs a lover who can inspire them to try and be a hero, if only to help the poor. And maybe to help the middle class.

Some heroes will be genius tutors who each tutor hundreds of millions.

And some leaders will be bad people who saw the light and became good, just like Scrooge, or Oscar Wilde's "The Unfriendly Giant."

Some people are like angels and play the hero to the downtrodden and depressed. They are heroes.

Many people will regard stars and Virtual stars as heroes. An inspiration to them. Including famous musicians for whom the people will go gaga. When Supercomputers come to make music, they will continue to go gaga only with the avatars of the computers: the Super Androids.

Some people will want to spend time with a hero but will often find the heroes are too busy for them and so will be heartbroken.

Some heroes try their best to succeed and never sell out but fail egregiously. It's just the way it is.

Some heroes will try to convince evil dictators to be more enlightened but will mostly fail and so will tend to become revolutionaries. Revolutionaries are often good people, but sometimes they are evil. Even evil people have their heroes.

The masses need to be educated by great geniuses who can see potential good citizens in them. Such geniuses would be heroes.

Some heroes are unsung and work behind the scenes to great effect.

Some heroes are rich philanthropists who help get millions out of poverty. In the future, with no more diseases, poor people will be better off anyway.

Some heroes will be a hero to some, an anathema to others. It's not cut and dried. But those who mean well are always welcome and adored by many.

Heroes tend to be altruists and kind and dedicated to helping others. New drugs will make one able to get extreme pleasure from doing good deeds.

Heroes will tend to burn out, rather than fade away. They will be serious and intense and walk a dangerous path.

Some heroes will be driven by goodness, others will be driven out of a sense of duty.

Some will want to get rich while helping others.

Some will be a hero to the elite and bring strong new policies to the forefront which will foster progress.

Many heroes will be ambassadors to the Supercomputers and Superhumans and will represent the people well.

Some heroes will themselves be Superhuman and will educate and give brain apps to the people to help them catch up.

THE PAST

Everyone should study more history and then apply the lessons learned to one's future life. But some futuristic realities didn't happen in history. So imagine what to do and do it.

And archaeology suggests modern humans have been around for millions of years. But just like lions and tigers they can all interbreed. Only lions and tigers will just attack one another.

In the past nearly everyone was rural and small village gossip would mean that everyone knew what everyone else was doing. So Big Brother is nothing new.

The oldest evidence of beer now comes from 11,000 or more years ago. Perhaps civilization was first created to grow crops for booze.

Ancient Greece teaches us that synergy of intellects can yield great dividends in democracies, like ancient Athens. And city states will be everywhere. And will be inspirational just like the late 1960's was inspirational, with the moon landing and peace and drugs and free love. Only in the near future, it will be MRT, eternal youth, great love drugs and so on.

Hero of Alexandria invented steam power in the first century A.D. But no one could see the use of it. Sometimes in history people are ahead of their time and go unrecognized, like a lot of writers for example.

The Fall of Rome is full of instances of debauchery and brutal entertainment and debauchery will come again and will lead to ruin for some. And brutal entertainment in action movies and UFC fighting and no rules barred fighting. Brawling like in hockey in the 1970's will come back and spread to other sports. The gladiators will return some day.

China's history shows that beauty and grace are golden. One Emperor after another followed the Confucian system which made fealty to the Emperor paramount. The Great Emperor will come again one day to Earth and/or Space.

India's history shows that it is hard to govern the whole Indian subcontinent with only 1 leader. And India has been saddled with the caste system and an antiquated religion which have held the country back. And Bollywood movies are just ordinary people dancing and singing ordinary songs. India can do much better.

Africa's history shows, it seems, that the first people originated from there. And in history Africa was plagued by wars and slave dealing. Now finally in the 21st century, the African economies are starting to grow, and the outlook is positive. They should find a way to use solar panels to power their civilizations.

Contact between the Americas and Asia and Europe must have taken place in ancient times. For example, the Aztec legends talked of a white man who would be their savior. And they mined gold and silver but not iron, which is odd. As if the white man had ordered them to produce gold and silver. And people came to Easter Island. They must have therefore found the Americas many times over.

Medieval times show us how a few of the elite can control everyone, keeping almost everyone in virtual slavery, while they live like Kings.

Britain ruled the seas and proved sea power was more important than land power. And Britain set up the people of the United States which had the most democratic system in history beginning in 1776 and improving after that.

Napoleon was a war monger but set up the middle class in France. To this day the middle class decides on leaders.

Hitler was a populist leader who appealed to anti-Semitic sentiments and making Germany the strongest World power. Once elected he dismissed German Intelligence and so there was no one to put a check on him. And he abandoned democracy and dissent. He was a one man show and almost obliterated the World. Imagine if Hitler had won?

In the past we had slaves, now we have wage slaves in most places. Some things never change.

Ford said, "History is bunk." But if people don't learn the lessons of history, they will suffer in the modern day. But many people are ignorant and will never learn. But for most, history should be paramount to a good education. Everything has a history.

History tells us, that sometimes were good, other times bad. Mostly people of the past lived in Dystopias that were very far from perfect. And the future promises to also be a Dystopia with machines taking over and people having no use. Superfluous people...

In history there were many, particularly the late 20th century, who wanted a free ride in life. And by 2100 there will be many who just live off the State and let the machines do the work. Some say it is a great revolution, others complain there is no role for them in the script.

In history, different ethnic groups attacked one another and, in many cases, wiped whole peoples out in genocidal killings. It was and always has been dog eat dog. And genocide continues to this day. Hopefully in the future they will put a stop to genocide using UW troops more actively than the UN peacekeepers of today.

History shows us that there is always abuse of certain groups. And such people would be looked down upon. In the future there will be many philosophies that people fight about. So, it will be genocide against intellectuals of differing types.

It seems to us today that history was a nightmare on the whole. But now many people say there is hope at the end of the tunnel. And hope for true Utopias.

In history, everyone who wasn't a white anglo-saxon male was persecuted in many "free," countries. Now they are trying to redress the wrongs. But there are always new wrongs occurring. In the future androids and holograms will be enslaved and punished just for being who they are. And people who don't keep pace with technology will be forgotten and/or abused.

Throughout history plague, smallpox, tuberculosis and many other diseases were always just a heartbeat away. So, people lived for the day as much as they could, but life was mostly hard work on the farm, for the vast majority.

In history many people had arranged marriages. This was another bane of history. Even love was not possible.

In history, different ethnic groups fought wars against one another, often. Add this together with disease as well as death during childbirth; it kept the population down. And there were times of famine and drought. The horrors.

In history, there were wars in which only the grunts died, and it was rare for officers to die. But the grunts marched to war, without questioning it.

Gordon Lightfoot sang, "In times best forgot, there was peace, there was not." Maybe it is best to learn about history, and then forget it and start with a clean slate.

FREEDOM

People who say they are free are often not... The wisdom that comes with freedom seldom leads to bragging.

They say children are free, but to grow up is to be freer.

Don't confuse lust with love. Lust is liberty and health; love can be a nightmare.

Crazy love gives more liberty than ordinary love.

Conventional wisdom is old people's wisdom. It won't usually lead to freedom.

If you surround yourself with people that are unlike you, you may learn a lot about life.

To have a lot of knowledge can make you free, but only if you really know how to use it... Trial and error is not the best way. Using your imagination is better...

One of the worst things that can happen to a free person is to lose freedom due to the rule of a cruel tyrant... But you can always go elsewhere....

In the country of the blind, no one is king. And no one is free.

Some say freedom is not for everyone. But everyone wants more freedoms if you talk to them.

It is good to be free in your mind, but it is better to be also free where you live.

If you truly live free many people will call you crazy. Anything unusual that people don't understand they will call crazy.

To be free you need to change constantly.

Some people say we are all living a lie. But everyone has a different idea of what kind of lie it is.

Money can buy you a lot of freedom and success. But a lot of rich people are not free at all and a lot of poor people are free...

Some say wanting freedom too much is a kind of greed... But greed can be good.

Surround yourself with free people and you will never despair...

Don't waste time trying to make stubborn people free. People are either open-minded or they are not.

Better to have never known freedom than to have had it only to lose it.

Sometimes people put a price on freedom or getting to be free requires a great sacrifice.

It is true that fools rush in, but it is also true that geniuses rush in before anyone else... Great thinkers are always looking at things that are free to rush into; some say it is passion...

Most people want peace, but many who seek power want war. It only takes one to ruin everyone's freedom.

Some people have too much free time and get into many bad habits.

Many people on the road to freedom love to make mistakes.

Children need to be taught to struggle for freedom and they need to be given lots of adversity. Otherwise, they will be spoiled.

In the future there will be new freedoms that we cannot even conceive of today.

They went to the moon and "proved" there was nothing in space. Even today few people can think of any use for the moon. Maybe put all the crazy people there...

There's no greater freedom than advanced thinking.

Some say imagination is more important than freedom. But more accurately imagination is only possible if you can free your mind. Creativity is freedom to do.

Many people think the world is getting crazier. But sometimes crazy situations can be very interesting, and one has freedom to be crazy; good crazy.

Early to bed and early to rise makes Jack a dull boy.

If you stay in one place too long you will have cabin fever… And lack freedom.

Some say ignorance is one kind of bliss, but freedom is a much more blissful experience.

People who fight for freedom should be praised and abetted in any way possible.

There are many fish in the sea but, some places have much better fishing than others… "Freedom to fish," is what matters.

It's a true fact that today progress is the "religion" of many free people. Much of the progress is due to scientists being free to develop our world.

It is of course natural to fear death… But don't fear death so much you can't live free.

Some think that sometimes hatred can be a noble emotion. And it can be noble, for example, to hate a ruthless tyrant. But many future Worlds people will likely not be free to hate their leader or hate their own lifestyle; if they do, they will be sent to Rehab.

It's not a bad thing to be bored. It makes us think more about life.

There's a fine line between freedom and slavery. Today many people work like slaves…

In a crazy world, the crazy people are the leaders.

Kind people are likely to make you freer than others. Don't underestimate a kind heart.

Some people are tragic figures who are destined to be not free and unhappy.

Life is just not a very inspiring period for some people these days… Free love has yet to return.

Sometimes illusions can be fun. Sometimes illusions are better than the truth… In the future free World, you can feel free to have illusions.

Some people are freethinkers, but they lose themselves along the way; after all, there are no footprints in the sand for us in this modern world... They have freedom but they make mistakes.

In the past people's greed was limited by their imagination. But some people today have no limit to their imagination or their greed... It's a crazy kind of freedom.

Today the greedy people think they own the world, but all they have is material things, which any wise person knows are largely unnecessary. But they don't want communism and want the freedom to pursue material things.

Perhaps the happiest people are those, who in old age, can say they've made a difference... And had the liberty to do so.

If you are not free maybe you could try moving to another city or country and start all over again. Sometimes all we need is a fresh start...

Freedom can be an addiction, like anything else. But if you are addicted to freedom, it might be a good thing.

Everyone knows that jail is a bad place. It is a place where no one has any freedom... But some people like it there as they don't have to do anything... For them jail can be a paradise...

Some people feel so free that they feel guilty looking at others who are not free. But it is very hard to change the World alone.

Some people are so afraid of mistakes that they are paralyzed and unable to do anything.

Some would play the fiddle while society went down... Let's face it all civilizations last for only a limited time... There are so many things or people that could bring ruin to us all... It just makes liberty all the more precious.

We went from a civilization that was basically based on slavery (the past) to one that is based more and more on freedom and dreams and wishes. Kind of like going from a terrible type of world to a great type...

What if you could be truly free to put yourself in another person's shoes; e.g., through MRT, would this change your outlook, or would you still be the same person? Maybe some day in the far future, they will be able to swap minds...

Maybe one day they will print money and give everyone in the country millions of dollars. And inflation would be kept at zero. Would that make people freer?

Don't expect to find totally free people in ordinary places: they will be mostly in very large cities or in places way off the beaten track...

Some homeless people refuse shelter as they only care about being free...

We need bad people to create adversity: something for us to struggle with to try and find liberty.

If you had the liberty to use MRT and read everyone's minds, you'd likely believe the human race is completely mad.

Some say to be totally free, would be God-like. Who knows maybe scientists are already working on it?

If you are free, you should seek political office and help your country to be more liberated... Especially in developing nations... Why not give it a shot?

In the future many people will regard the real world as cruel and be cruel themselves... tough love they call it. But there is little doubt that the future will be kinder than the past. At least there will be less violence... Or so it would seem...

Some people say liberty is to have nothing to do... But there is a lot of good work to be done in this world...

Conversation with someone who lacks imagination is not much fun... Many people get sick of parties and conversations and so settle down... They blame the world for being boring when actually, it is they themselves that are boring.... But perhaps in the future people would not be given the freedom of being boring. Brain apps and hypnosis will be given to boring people.

Some people say they are searching for meaning as well as freedom... Of course, meaning will prove elusive, but freedom is real and can be assessed...It is relatively easy to strive for freedom... Others say happiness is where it's at, but this is also elusive... Better to just be as free as you can be and see what happens...

Freedom can be a virtue; many of the freest type people are virtuous at heart... freedom is good...

Some people dislike the human race on the whole, but some of these people are great thinkers... As elite thinkers they have the freedom to avoid most people, most of whom are mediocre.

If the world was to suddenly end for you, for example a rare car accident, would you really be happy with your life...? If not, you could have back-up clones whom you shared memories with every day to the point where one couldn't tell the difference. Such people would be emancipated from worrying about death.

Some would say telling the truth indicates a lot of finesse; but many people are great liars... Of course it is nice if you don't have to lie, but most people demand to hear what they want to hear... But in the future people will not be free to lie. Neo lie detectors will see to that. The truth is liberating.

Some areas of this world are very dangerous, but since there are few tourists in such places you can be free to have a lot of fun meeting the locals...

Racism, sexism and other kinds of discrimination are disappearing... It kind of looks like a future of peace and stability... But there will be new problems in the future that we can only guess about, e.g. some people will be too free and upset the status quo... and cabin fever will drive many in Space insane. But one would be free to do their very best in life in the near future in most places.

Some people are like beautiful flowers... They are beautiful and that's it... They say things like, Isn't beauty enough for people? But most free people will be open-minded and won't be satisfied with pure beauty.

Just who are the best people? Everyone disagrees... And they will never agree... But some clever people need to seize the bull by the horns and take control of this World. And they need to institute tests for intelligence and wisdom and kindness for would-be World leaders. Freedom created by the elite.

The freedom to access eternal youth will be a lifesaver for most. Others will live on the edge of sanity.

If MRT is allowed, people might be entertained by "thought debates" in which people would have no shame... and reveal their innermost thoughts... But MRT would make people free.

The freedom to love anyone you wish will be highly valued by future people.

It is likely that women in the future will feel they have something to prove and will end up richer than men... Women will be truly emancipated.

There are many kinds of freedom... But politics is a very dangerous subject for a free person...

Sometimes people feel free doing nothing at all... They say that life is like riding a wild bull for most people and they themselves prefer peace and quiet....

Everyone knows that freedom is valuable. Maybe in the future people will be judged as to how free they are (MRT etc.). And people will be desperate to become freer and hence improve their status.

Actually, one day everyone will be free and then people will cease to talk about it: it will be a given.

For free people, old age is as fun as youth.

Sooner or later everyone on this Earth will likely be free. But what will they focus on then? Perhaps they will think creativity is the thing to strive for... And if they become creative, maybe the next step is to try and be a Superhuman.

How many people can truly know about freedom...? It is undoubtedly a small number... Sometimes it may seem like an esoteric cult....

Happiness goes to the ones who are lucky some would say... But it is more likely that happiness comes only from freedom...

Some people go to the grave laughing their heads off with marijuana and laughing gas... It is a good way to be, but hard to mimic in practice... Freedom to die is a valuable freedom.

If you want to be free you have to pay the price. Sometimes, in some situations, it seems the price is too high, so go somewhere else...

In the future perhaps city states will be the freest form of government.

It is not enough to say you believe in freedom but rather you need to show clever free people how free you are...

If you believe you can change the world start with easy ways like helping the poor and then graduating to help eliminate poverty worldwide... It is easy for you to make thousands of people free... If not more...

No one knows about the maximum freedom... But there do seem to be limits... But in the future, for some people, there will be no limits and people will feel free to do anything they want....

ABOUT THE AUTHOR

Tom Ball holds a B.A. in archaeology and a B.S. in geography. He has travelled to 35 countries and lived in six. His favorite country is Taiwan. He works as an online English teacher and volunteers as co-founder for fleasonthedog.com, a literary e-zine. He has written 32 books, most of which have been published, at least in part. He now resides in Ontario, Canada.

www.ingramcontent.com/pod-product-compliance
Lightning Source LLC
Chambersburg PA
CBHW072005110526
44592CB00012B/1209
* 9 7 8 1 9 4 5 8 2 4 4 9 4 *